IntechOpen

Supporting open minds since 2005

Sustainability Concept in Developing Countries
http://dx.doi.org/10.5772/intechopen.82946
Edited by Surendra N. Kulshreshtha

Contributors
Abimbola Asojo, Babatunde Jaiyeoba, Anissa Frini, Sarah Benamor, Bruno Urli, Phoebe Koundouri, Lydia Papadaki, Mohammad, Ana Paola Balderrama Carmona, Norma Patricia Silva Beltran, Edgar Felipe Moran Palacio, Norma Patricia Adan Bante, Luis Alberto Zamora Alvarez, Henrik Haller, Anders Jonsson, Ginnette Flores-Carmenate, Sunil Kulkarni

First published in London, United Kingdom, 2020 by IntechOpen
IntechOpen is the global imprint of INTECHOPEN LIMITED, registered in England and Wales, registration number: 11086078, 7th floor, 10 Lower Thames Street, London, EC3R 6AF, United Kingdom
Printed in Croatia

British Library Cataloguing-in-Publication Data
A catalogue record for this book is available from the British Library

Additional hard and PDF copies can be obtained from orders@intechopen.com

Sustainability Concept in Developing Countries
Edited by Surendra N. Kulshreshtha
p. cm.
Print ISBN 978-1-83880-472-5
Online ISBN 978-1-83880-473-2
eBook (PDF) ISBN 978-1-78985-855-6

For EU product safety concerns:
IN TECH d.o.o., Prolaz Marije Krucifikse Kozulić 3, 51000 Rijeka, Croatia, info@intechopen.com or visit our website at intechopen.com.

Meet the editor

Surendra N. Kulshreshtha is currently a professor in the Department of Agricultural and Resource Economics at the University of Saskatchewan, Saskatoon, a position he has held for the past 51 years. He received his initial education in India, coming to Canada to get a PhD in Agricultural Economics from the University of Manitoba. He has been a Visiting Scientist at the International Institute for Applied Systems Analysis at Laxenburg, Austria; Virginia Polytechnique and State University; Agriculture and Agri-Food Canada; and McGill University. He has also participated in several overseas projects in Indonesia, Zambia, and India through the Canadian International Development Agency, and has been an invited participant at several FAO and United Nations Environmental Program activities.

Contents

Preface

As a simple interpretation, sustainability can be described as either a process or a state that can be maintained at a certain level for as long as it is wanted. The term is associated with that proposed by the Bruntland Commission as "Sustainable Development," which is defined as development that "meets the needs of the present without compromising the ability of future generations to meet their own needs." Thus, "sustainability" is the study of how natural systems function, remain diverse, and produce everything they need for the ecology to remain in balance. However, in addition to natural resources, we also need social and economic resources; sustainability is not just environmentalism. Maintaining sustainability in any economic system is very important, and even more so in the context of developing countries. This book presents some case studies and methodological issues with a focus on developing countries. Part 1 includes studies on conceptual frameworks related to sustainability as well as methodologies relevant to its investigation. Part 2 includes case studies dealing with sustainability applications. Chapter 1 is a description of the people-centered social totality approach, which was applied to low-income housing policy. Since sustainability has three pillars (economic, social, and environmental), use of a multi-criteria decision-making tool is very appropriate. Chapter 2 examines such a tool. Chapter 3 presents an integration of the water-food-energy nexus, since natural resources are used for more than one purpose in an economic system requiring their integration. Chapter 4 examines the use of natural resources in rural areas, using herbicides as a case study. Part 2 begins with Chapter 5, which describes the issue of governance. Chapter 6 describes some of the activities that might lead to sustainability, and finally, Chapter 7 provides a description of sustainability status. The editor hopes that contributions would be of some interest not only for professional in developing countries but also in developed countries.

Dr. Surendra N. Kulshreshtha
University of Saskatchewan,
College of Agriculture and Bioresources,
Department of Agricultural and Resource Economics,
Saskatoon, Canada

Section 1

Concepts and Methods

Chapter 1

A People-Centred Social Totality Approach to Low-Income Housing in the Developing World

E. Babatunde Jaiyeoba and Abimbola O. Asojo

Abstract

In a significant part of the developing world, especially sub-Saharan Africa, public housing policies and implementation have depended on a top-to-bottom approach in an attempt to ensure housing supply. However, public authorities sometimes backed by international agencies preferring to operate through the housing market have failed to meet the housing need, especially for low-income people. Even when the users are involved like in the slum dwellers association, the organisation of the process is majorly controlled by the public authorities. While government and public institutions attained minimal success in housing provision for the lowest classes in the society, the people have been more successful in housing production. This chapter situates the housing problem and policy responses in the context of the developing world characterised by limited capacity to control and manage the largely more successful informal people-controlled housing production structure. A cyclic people-centred strategy framework for low-income housing is proposed based on town-gown collaboration in studying low-income people, their activated housing process and the houses produced to guide present strategies and synthesise future strategies and policy. This framework emanates from Henri Lefebvre's social totality explanation to understand how low-income people negotiate housing from the social context.

Keywords: low income, housing strategy, developing world, social totality

1. Introduction

Housing policy is naturally a top-down process since government should be seen or at least perceived as taking care of all the people in any country. The mode of carrying out this laudable ideal of ensuring housing provision for all citizens irrespective of income varies in different contexts depending on the housing policy-success-failure history, objectives set, the desires and mode of government in place.

This chapter examines housing strategies in the developing world, especially for low-income people in sub-Saharan Africa. It x-rays the housing problem in the developing world and policy prescriptions vis-a-vis the housing solutions of low-income people. Whereas public authority approaches have limited success in housing supply, cross sections of low-income people in the developing world have succeeded in housing production in informal ways. It is important to understand how these low-income people succeed to device housing strategies that work for the poor. The social totality concept derivable from Lefebvre's theory of space provides an explanation of how these low-income people negotiate housing from the social context [1, 2]. The concept is also examined and the relations with housing discussed to illustrate how housing strategies can be synthesised from understanding the housing process of low-income people in different contexts. The literature review is international to situate the housing situation in a global perspective since many housing strategies in the developing world emanate directly or indirectly from the developed world. The United Nations, the World Bank and other global agencies, consultants, researchers and professionals from different regions of the world in the spirit of globalisation are understandably active in recommending policies and solutions to the housing problem in the developing world. The conventional solution is that government and private sector are expected to be major actors in housing supply.

Formal housing provision by government and or private organisations have direct beneficiaries: families who possess the willingness and ability to buy from the market, consultants, contractors, skilled and unskilled workmen in the construction industry, loan and credit institutions, building material producers and allied industries [3]. Public housing estates are known to be large homogenous enclaves of poverty in unattractive locations but are justified by supply side political idealists for affordable housing [4]. The political ideals that shape public housing are related to the political, social, legal and economic indices of different countries. Significantly, private housing and informal housing in different contexts are affected by the same factors with the people at the centre of the ping pong impacts of these different factors. The peoples housing is the product of their reaction and manipulation of these different factors to attain a human life necessity. Low-income housing covers between 60 and 80% of towns' and cities' developed land areas in Africa, Asia, Latin America and the Caribbean and accounts for 50–70% of the fixed capital formation of urban areas (UN-Habitat, 2003). In spite of this, there is a wide gap between supply and demand of low-income housing. Obviously, strategies that alleviate low-income housing problem will also contribute to the development efforts of these developing countries.

The goal of housing strategy for low-income housing as stated for public housing should be to ensure that the disadvantaged have decent, affordable housing through political support and policy [4]. This goal has been difficult to achieve in most developing countries. For example, most of the houses built for the poor, which constitute only 4% of the housing stock, in Ghana ended up with the middle-income group; the growing private sector only build for high-income groups, while the informal sector accounts for 90% of the housing stock [5]. Actually, low-income people who need housing should be the anchor point of studies to redirect housing policies and strategies. The people who have succeeded in what public authorities, private corporations, international organisations, and their collaborations whether Public Private Participation (PPP) or International Institutions Assisted Programmes have failed in should be studied. Their profile, individual and communal, the process they adopted, the different stages of the product and how this profile, process and product are continually defined and negotiated in the social context need to be understood to synthesise appropriate housing strategies for low-income people. Studying low-income people with the conceptual viewpoint of social totality that builds upon the idea of everything in space including housing as socially produced will help to overcome the housing challenge in the developing world.

2. Housing challenges in the developing world

The housing situation in the developing world is presently worrisome, and the prospects of escalation of the problem are obvious considering that most of the urban population increase in the world, in fact 95%, will be in the developing world [6]. The quantitative deficit in housing has been escalating: 650 million in 1990, 760 million in 2000 and 863 million in 2014 [7, 8].

The housing inadequacy of the developing world is such that the UN-Habitat 2015 report documents 880 million living in slums against 792 million in 2000 [9]. This fact among others may have informed the integration of 'housing for all' target towards 2030 in the Sustainable Development Goals [10]. Urbanisation in the developing countries is often associated with increasing concentration of 'slums', a term that is so generally employed that more than half of the settlements in a few large urban centres may be so classified. It reflects how bad the housing situation in the cities of the developing world is. Globally, there was an increase of 14% in the number of people living in slums in cities across the world between 2000 and 2014 [6]. Most of these slums are habitat to low-income people in the developing world.

The classification of most low-income housing areas as slums is one that has been debated often since the John Turner studies [8–10] in Latin America that highlight the immense resources possessed and expended on the production of the existing housing by poor people [11–13]. Also, a lot of capital is locked up in these settlements that could be tapped into through regularisation and legalisation [14]. It is significant that in parts of the developing world, unlike the squatter settlements in Latin America, most houses produced by the low-income are not necessarily 'illegal' in the sense that the land is purchased and there were attempts by the producers to legalise the process.

Quantitatively speaking, the housing problem may have disappeared after the industrial revolution with mass production techniques, but economists argue that there are competing sectors and uses for the limited and scarce resources of countries. Countries in the developing world have more limited resources that are unreasonably mismanaged to exclude more proportion of citizens from housing solutions. It was therefore convenient for governments in these countries to adopt the enabling shelter strategy as advocated in Global Shelter Strategies in the 1990s and put together in UN and World Bank reports. The philosophy was for government to tactically withdraw from housing provision and housing subsidy, manage institutional, legislative and regulatory environment as part of the economy but empower the private sector and the housing market to produce housing for all [15].

The enabling strategy has been largely unsuccessful for low-income housing since houses meant for them have been taken up by higher income groups due to lower housing production, lack of institutional infrastructure, non-transparency of the housing market in the midst of more social, economic and environmental exclusion and therefore growing numbers of the poor in inadequate housing or homeless [15–18].

The housing problem in the developing world is not only quantitative, it is associated with rapid urbanisation in poorly managed economies and inequitable distribution of wealth exacerbating poverty and therefore housing affordability. In the case of Africa, urbanisation is not associated with industrialisation (except in Johannesburg, South Africa) which means that it does not translate to higher wages like in Europe and Asia. Rather, things are more expensive with people spending more for daily needs such as food, water, electricity and other sources of power. An experiential survey shows that the rental value of minimal accommodation may account for up to 40–60% of gross income in big cities [19]. Developing nations are also bedevilled with political, religious and other developmental problems that mask and divert attention from the actual problems including housing. There are policies on paper to address these main problems, but the implementation falls short of the goal, objectives and targets due to inadequate database, manpower, technological resources, and especially financial resources sometimes related to unaccountable resource allocation. In addition, developing countries especially in sub-Saharan Africa feature high level of informality in the economy. Many activities in the informal sector occur outside the radar of public authorities, institutions and agencies and are therefore not accounted for in government balance sheets of production, consumption nor taxation. This informal sector is where most low-income people work. By contrast, the governance, urban planning and economy are controlled by diverse and fragmented actors and formal and informal processes in the public, private and civic sectors. Navigating these complex institutions is accomplished depending on the level of power; in principle, low-income people are the lowest in the ladder of power considering their level of political exclusion.

Furthermore, in most developing countries, there is a lack of political will, resources and manpower for futuristic planning, especially for urban areas. This results in the continued use of outdated and colonial era planning laws, regulations and building codes. Also, when there are new laws, there is a lack of capacity, equipment and manpower to enforce these laws and associated regulations. Even formal developments lack access to adequate, properly located land as was the case in Raipur, India [3]. Also, too much land is consumed by adhering to regulation that increases 'generosity' of land use in low density, generous parking, setbacks, air space in between buildings causing urban sprawl, high land, service and infrastructure costs [3]. Sometimes ownership and control of land for housing are still contested between traditional authorities and different levels of government. For example, Nigeria has a land use decree that vests the power to release land for development on the state governors [20]. This position sometimes sets the federal institutions against the state ones and both against traditional family-owned property owners for housing development. Most informal developments are therefore at the outskirts of cities where land costs are cheaper and development control is weaker making it possible to continue construction with or without planning permit or approval or where extremely high standard regulations are yet to be enforced. The outskirt of cities is poorly served with infrastructure since the cost of servicing the urban areas itself is already so high that government is just managing to cope, if they are coping at all. Politics, power play and election success are interwoven with the formal and informal housing provision processes. This is most prominent in situations of illegal occupation of urban land, squatters and slums as it relates to Latin America, Asia and a few very large urban areas in Africa. In the Raphur case study in India, new clientelism has replaced the old clientelism of feudal lords where the slum dwellers bargain with politicians, political office holders and political parties for goods, services, protection and individual needs in contrast to systemic changes with the promise of political support during elections [3]. Also, slum dwellers are said to have realised that their vote is the source of power to bargain with politicians and possibly build outside the law.

Political motivation and segregation which were overriding factors in early public housing in the twentieth century in United States and European countries in large urban projects are being repeated now in developing countries. Finished houses are being built for the housing market to be purchased at sometimes subsidised rates and with loan, mortgage or other forms of formal credit, often in uninteresting locations. The merits of finished houses built by the private, public and the public-private sectors are many. They provide houses with standardised plans and basic services in a more efficient and systematic way than the incremental process adopted by many private housing producers. Necessarily such housing can only be acquired through mortgage, loan and credit schemes often associated with some form of subsidy for either the provider or the consumer or both. Apart from the financial inefficiency and inequities that subsidies allow, there is also inequity in access to loan and credit schemes by those in the formal and informal sectors and the type and location of housing that can be purchased. Using provident fund as the source of finance is known to have accentuated the global financial crises in 2008 and gave birth to repetitive, standardised soulless housing on the outskirts of cities without other necessary uses critical for healthy living [21].

These projects featured a homogenous sector of the population in unattractive locations that later degenerated into slums and concentrations of poverty [22–24]. While the recent development of mixed tenure is not being adopted in the most recent projects, especially in Sub-Saharan Africa, however, public/private partnerships and more private developers are involved in delivering greater mix of typologies. The new millennium and post global financial crisis and the resulting demand for affordable housing made these countries, especially Western Europe, utilise the urban-diversity approach with all of its merits as a response to past mistakes [25]. The estates are diverse in terms of people (ethnicity, income, age) and land uses [25]. Negative effects are known to arise from urban diversity in public housing estates which may not be true about privately developed areas. Not learning from history seems to be a problem with respect to housing strategies in the developing world, especially sub-Saharan Africa.

3. Housing policy responses in the developing world

Many approaches to alleviating the housing problem are being taken in different parts of the world and the Latin American experience has always been in focus since the John Turner studies in the 1960s. These studies brought to the fore an awareness of the immense resources possessed by people as individuals or community in housing. The political implications of this in relation to distribution of power and control at the local, national and global levels are a continuous debate among the political left, right and the non-aligned. Turners exposes were in the context of Latin America where group illegal invasion, occupation and building of houses in rapidly urbanising cities became the norm in the middle of the twentieth century and the political leadership and the then East-West divide ignited housing-political debates.

Government assistance in housing production and housing finance as implemented in Argentina, Brazil, Colombia and Mexico and government-subsidised new housing production coupled with slum improvements in India and South Africa [8]. The slum dwellers association in Thailand, India, South Africa and other places attempts to collectivise housing solution efforts for housing and the necessary infrastructure.

The World Bank's intention of making the private sector to invest in low-income housing by demonstrating public assistance for private housing, cost recovery, replicability and profitability in sites-and-services schemes and slum upgrading in the 1970s through self-help efforts did not materialise [10, 26, 27]. Limitations of sites-and-services schemes include: wrong location on the outskirts of cities because of lower cost of land but resulting in separation of occupants from the job market and their social networks, lack of infrastructure and high costs of later service and infrastructure connection. In fact, on this basis, many of these schemes had low initial uptake and some remained under developed [28]. Also, impossibly high planning standards and unaffordable construction standards beyond the unusual for low-income housing are imposed. The subsequent evaluation of these projects was also short term without consideration of the usual construction period of between 15 and 20 years of incremental construction of low-income people. These projects were pronounced unsuccessful, discredited and abandoned too early. The evaluation was also based on the quality of the different transitional levels of the houses and the end product, which in many ways resembles the informally produced private housing [29]. Government-supported projects are also said to be cumbersome to administer according to the donor agencies including the World Bank. They were regarded as unconventional and by the early 1990s the World Bank started withdrawing support for such projects including the sites-and-services schemes [20, 22].

Another policy response is for low-income estates or affordable housing to be built as a means of increasing housing provision for low-income people. Whenever the private sector or the public-private sector puts a housing estate in the market as low-income estate, especially with the Nigerian experience, it is predominantly occupied or commodified by higher income groups.

There is a perception within the professional circles that the low-income need single family-dwelling typology desired by educated middle- and high-income people because of the prevailing emphasis on nuclear family over the extended family. As confirmed in Ghana, and also common in Nigeria, multi-habited houses rented or owned are the predominant house type of urban low-income households [30, 31]. This perception is what accounts for the typology of buildings made available in the housing market in the developing world, especially sub-Saharan Africa.

The latest effort of 'natural resource-backed financial deals for the provision of infrastructure and housing' in sub-Saharan Africa with Democratic Republic of Congo (DRC), Kenya and Nigeria as examples was examined by Quigley [32]. These efforts are geared towards creating massive estates on the outskirts of towns with funds sourced externally from other places, especially China. Far-reaching questions are being raised concerning these efforts including not understanding the historical context of policy [32]. Furthermore, these efforts rarely improve housing affordability and access to the needy and are out of tune with urban planning, especially sustainability and inclusiveness. Therefore, effective housing solutions and inclusive urbanisation should be sought in a broader understanding of the policy, regulatory and urban planning environment and income levels in the context [8].

Also, a better understanding of the equity effects of the housing strategy financialisaton in the developing world is necessary. Global interactions with country-specific local institutions, structures, agents and housing outcomes need to be understood in the search for alternative international housing policies not dominated by finance [10]. Above all, formal authorities should respect and seek understanding of how low-income people cross the barrier to becoming 'landlords'—a term that signifies success in housing production.

4. Housing strategies of the low income

The poor and the low income in various places have different housing strategies peculiar to their needs, degree of exclusion and contextually determined ability to pay for housing. Many have argued that the rental mode of tenure is the most appropriate for the low income [33]. However, in a situation where even that mode is not being considered by government and its institutions, low-income households have to solve their own housing problem. Whatever tenure status is preferred anyway, public authorities lack the data and the wherewithal to provide. The low income has found a way of fending for themselves either as landlord (owned housing and provider of rental housing), tenant, through shared accommodation or squat in any available private or public physical space. The generic term 'slums' is interchangeably used for these different housing strategies of the poor resulting in the distinguishing characteristics of these strategies being lost [34]. The challenges of accessing rental accommodation in a context where private 'shylock' landlords and caretakers—informal estate agents—rule the market are many. Rental accommodation remains in short supply due to lack of financial support either from the public or private sector and sometimes due to rent control laws. Rent control laws discourage present providers from further investing in new or maintaining properties [35–37]. This causes a shortage of rental accommodation relative to demand. Many landlords who are bent on buying a new land or continue incremental construction of another building for rent sometimes aided by the estate agents who may have their own objective of maximising returns through legal and illegal commissions ask for advance of 1 year or more yearly rent. This makes it very difficult for low-income people to put together the rent since it amounts to many months of income assuming there are no necessary expenditures like food for the family, transportation, education and health costs, among others. In a case study, those that cross this hurdle in Ghana were found to do so 'by the Grace of God', friend and family support considering their irregular income that makes it difficult to pay monthly rent [4]. In another case study in Nigeria deploying multidimensional explanations of Lefebvre's theory of space describes how indigenous knowledge, residential history, culture of home ownership in the fatherland, motivation to be a landlord, provide for the family and be self-actualised were implicated when low-income people utilised multiple resources to negotiate housing from the context of Ibadan, Nigeria [31]. The motivation to have self-owned housing by the low income is high in the developing world since it is sometimes seen as a cultural imperative by some ethnic groups, especially with high rental, food and infrastructure costs coupled with generally expensive cost of living in the urban areas. For example, the Yorubas of Western Nigeria believe that if you simply soak cassava flour in cold water and eat in the corner of your own house, anybody can be made to believe the meal was an international cuisine or delicacy.

If renting is a tough task for low-income people, home ownership is more difficult. Public sector provision is negligible, mortgage system is either non-existent, non-functional or not realistic because of high interest rates due to the value of the local currency and other distortions in national economies. Also, only people in the public and organised private sector can meet the administrative requirements and the conditionalities for the mortgage. In addition, the low-income people that lack collateral in the formal sense and ability to follow up on the sometimes-cumbersome administrative processes do not qualify for other formal financing options like from commercial banks and similar agencies. Designers of low-income housing need to invent or reinvent their role in low-income housing provision to propose appropriate solutions [38]. Whereas public and private sector low-income or affordable housing in Nigeria is the nuclear, single-family 2- or 3-bedroom apartment, most low-income people actually build the rooming house. The typical house in a case study in Nigeria is six-room (41.1%) and eight-room (38.2%) rectangular, one-level house (90.1%) with shared bathroom, toilet and cooking spaces grouped together at the back. This typology is a product of multiple considerations including their residential history [38]. The modal group (29.8%) started construction the same year land was bought and majority (61.5%) started using the house within 3 years of starting construction with the mean duration being 4.62 years. The typology built is a transformation of the Yoruba vernacular house as described by earlier authors [39].

Generally, the middle- and high-income people in the case of Nigeria have since learnt that if you want to own a house you may have to do it through the private sector since the private sector produces 90% of housing [40]. The person will search for land through individual and family network depending on income, desired location and taste considering job location of the breadwinners of the family, the children's school and the proposed location of retirement. The house is also planned to be self-sustaining in infrastructure—water supply, power supply, sewage and waste disposal. The overall financial demand makes income the overriding determinant of homeownership and the level of housing infrastructure.

The big question to be answered is: if the middle- and high-income groups are finding it difficult to access housing, how much more difficult can it be for the different categories of low-income people? To attempt a workable housing strategy for low-income people, how members of this group attained success in this regard in different contexts needs to be understood.

Whether owned or rental mode of tenure, the informal sector remains the most prominent housing provider in sub-Saharan Africa. In the case of Brazil and India, even the housing-enabling strategies and government provision are shrouded in misconceptions and a trial and error process. Debt management and structural adjustment programmes are part of the many challenges obscuring low-income housing policies in the Global South [15]. These misconceptions include that poor people need modern finished homes; more emphasis on the national economy boosting potential of housing construction and market; illusion that a conducive environment for private sector absorbing housing poverty in the housing market is in place and that there is sufficient public and civic participation in planning and decision making in the housing process. In the midst of these misconceptions in public authorities and private institutions housing provision, low-income people have been engaging the system and self-providing [41]. The concept of social totality explains how low-income people succeed in negotiating housing from the societal context.

5. The concept of social totality

Social totality as a concept emanates from the critical theory idea that social issues should not be isolated from the socio-historical processes and developments in the society, especially as a critique of capitalism now branded neoliberalism. It advocates that any attempt to explain and understand social phenomenon needs a broad theoretical framework that allows all social issues to be examined for analysis and critique. The Hegelian-Marxian concept of totality is often antagonised with its economic and political critic of capitalism as an exploitative and oppressive system to the working class that benefits only the rich without appreciating the merits of freedom and reward for innovation and creativity [35].

It is possible to analyse the different ways 'totality' is used in different contexts by critical theorists. In the critique of production processes in the capitalist political economy, 'totality' refers to the structure of the society and the economy that governs other aspects of social life. In the same vein, totality refers to the diachronic or historical perspective, which describes historical conditions before the present capitalist society and projected growth of capitalism in different contexts and possible indices for transition to socialism [42]. Totality allows theory and practice to dig deep beyond how social issues appear to different viewers into the disconnections and divisions in viewpoints within and without the issue to apprehend the reality. Totality is the avenue to comprehend reality as an interrelated whole to avoid partial and fragmented views of reality [43].

Overall, the whole idea is to avoid explanations that focus only on economic terms but trace linkages with the social, political, cultural and psychic in ways that dwarf the boundaries of knowledge reproduced by disciplinary fragmentation. As aptly put by Kellner, the implication of totality in critical theory to social theory is that,

> *'Social theory therefore involves construction of a model of the current society and a demonstration of the fundamental connections—as well as of the contradictions and conflicts—among the various domains of the current social system. Consequently, critical theory provides analyses of a mediated social totality that describe various relations among spheres of reality, rather than reducing all of society to the dynamics of the economy' [42].*

Lefebvre's theory of space is one of such social theories that believes in the interrelatedness of issues and the non-fragmentary approach to analysis of social issues including housing [44].

6. Lefebvre, social totality and housing

In Marxian analysis, the housing crisis emanates from the 'capital logic' that the state has competing problems deserving state resources so much that each need should be satisfied in a market approach in an environment enabled by government to allow private enterprise to flourish.

Lefebvre does not believe in the fragmentation of knowledge or disciplines in looking at social problems. Specialised categories of economics, philosophy, architecture, sociology, psychology, planning or history cannot confine totality of knowledge within its boundaries since totality is fragmented. The human beings that make up the society are in income classes with divisions in each class, the government and institutions are hierarchical and relative to housing there is public sector, private sector and partnerships between them. The real sector in informal housing can actually be described as non-public, non-private since it sometimes operates independently of both. Totality is in an unending transition with every aspect of life related to the total character of reality [45]. Many aspects of Lefebvre's theory of production of space have been thrown at housing with various interpretations, concepts and future research problems emanating. The contribution of Turner to informal development theory, sustainable development, participatory housing and architecture can be summarised by the title of his academic publications—'Freedom to Build' and 'Housing by People'. Also, Turner's challenge of assumptions of public authorities on control and social hierarchy at local and national levels is based on the dual questions 'who decides and who provides'. Turner's spontaneous housing advocacy and Lefebvre's all-embracing 'spatial appropriation of autogestion' gives an imperative to explore alternative relations between architectural practices, social relationships and global inequality [46]. Low-income housing provision and strategy can benefit a lot from this proposition.

Also, every aspect of modern life is in a crisis of change and transitions, in all sectors, which are all interrelated. In fact, crisis is both total and permanent [47]. Perhaps if low-income housing is defined as a crisis in the developing world like terrorism, natural disasters and climate change, more strategies that are people-centred would have come up. Production is reconceptualised beyond economics to include the built environment, artistic forms and the social relations of production in Lefebvre's conception of space. Abstract economic laws and social structures alone cannot explain production without human agency and human activities cannot be adduced to causes [48, 49]. The natural environment is slowly but surely converted by human beings to the built environment which includes housing and social relations is involved. Lefebvre provides explanations of how the built environment as a portion of space is produced by human agency and the social forces as social space—where space is both lived and produced [49, 50]. Housing as a substantial part of the built environment is therefore socially produced. Also, economic exclusion of low-income people is insufficient to understand the difficulty in accessing housing. The multidimensional exclusion can only be apprehended by considering social, economic, political, cultural, technological and financial issues, the relations between them and other emerging forces in the societal context. Therefore, to understand the problems of low-income housing access and negotiated production by successful low-income people, a social totality concept is required.

This chapter introduces a new perspective developed from Lefebvre's social theory of space in seeing housing as being socially produced in different contexts and needing a social totality concept to analyse and synthesise strategies that can guide people-centred solutions to low-income housing crisis in the developing world.

7. The way forward for housing strategies in the developing world

The prevailing idea is that adopting a variety of housing strategies is needed in the developing world to overcome the housing problem. However, these strategies should emanate from an understanding of the real housing need and the people's process as constrained by factors in the social context. For example, it was observed that China's urban housing policy is deficient in not assisting the rural to urban migrants who mostly live in slums though the central government is embarking on large-scale projects to house them. It was suggested that market-housing programmes such as enabling or self-help strategies, land reform and micro finance will have to be adapted to the Chinese context rather than direct comparison with similarly transitioning European countries since the context is different [51]. Context has long been established as critical to housing strategy and it is even more important in countries of the developing world where most housing is provided by the people with little or no support from government at all levels.

Understanding of specific locations, the low-income people's behaviour, priorities and housing standards and the informal housing process and success rate of policies on ground give better information than aggregate conditions given by UN-Habitat [8]. The World Bank's intention of building on the strength of the informal sector by the aided self-help projects of the 1950s and the sites-and-services schemes with upgrading schemes of the 1970s should have been preceded by social totality studies in different countries with the low-income people's housing process and product at the centre of it. A demand-driven housing strategy approach to prevent wrongly targeted and sometimes abandoned or uninhabited housing supply will reduce the housing crisis in the developing world. Also, there is an existing structure of housing provision that can be restructured by studying the constraints beyond identifying and addressing the supply and demand constraints and designing affordable housing markets. While policies try to address core economic principles with institutionally based market-enabling efforts, rules and procedures, they fail because actors and informal institutions in housing provision are not fully brought into view [3].

The social totality approach includes identifying low-income people who already initiated housing production, especially after acquiring land, started a foundation and belong to a community or home-based organisation. For example, in a Nigerian case study, the most difficult stages in the housing production process are land acquisition, foundation laying and roofing [26]. After overcoming the first two, low-income people that belong to home town organisations, community groups, skilled workers guild or union, trader's association and similar recognisable local organisations or cooperatives should be able to access a consolidated revolving credit. Their property, whatever state it is, and the local organisation or cooperative they belong to will be collateral for the credit. These same local organisations are well recognised by politicians during electioneering campaigns, especially close to election time. When the election is over and they are in political position and it is time to implement promises in their manifesto, they forget these organisations they exploited just to achieve their own end of winning elections.

This necessitates contextual studies working backwards from data collection on the field to data analysis in the administrative and academic offices before planning and housing strategies can evolve from the synthesis of analysed information. Planning and housing strategies are then implemented on the field and the cycle starts all over again as shown in **Figure 1**. This can only be possible with town and gown collaboration in the developing countries. Many disciplines in the design, planning and environmental field rarely collaborate on academics in the developing world and the schism between theory and practice is even more. Academics in educational institutions and practitioners on the field and in public institutions and authorities have to work together in this cyclic process for workable low-income housing strategies to continuously evolve until the situation improves.

The enabling approach as presently operated is focused on the housing market, especially the private sector, to deliver houses and make positive contribution to the economy at different levels. This approach has to be redirected at individuals

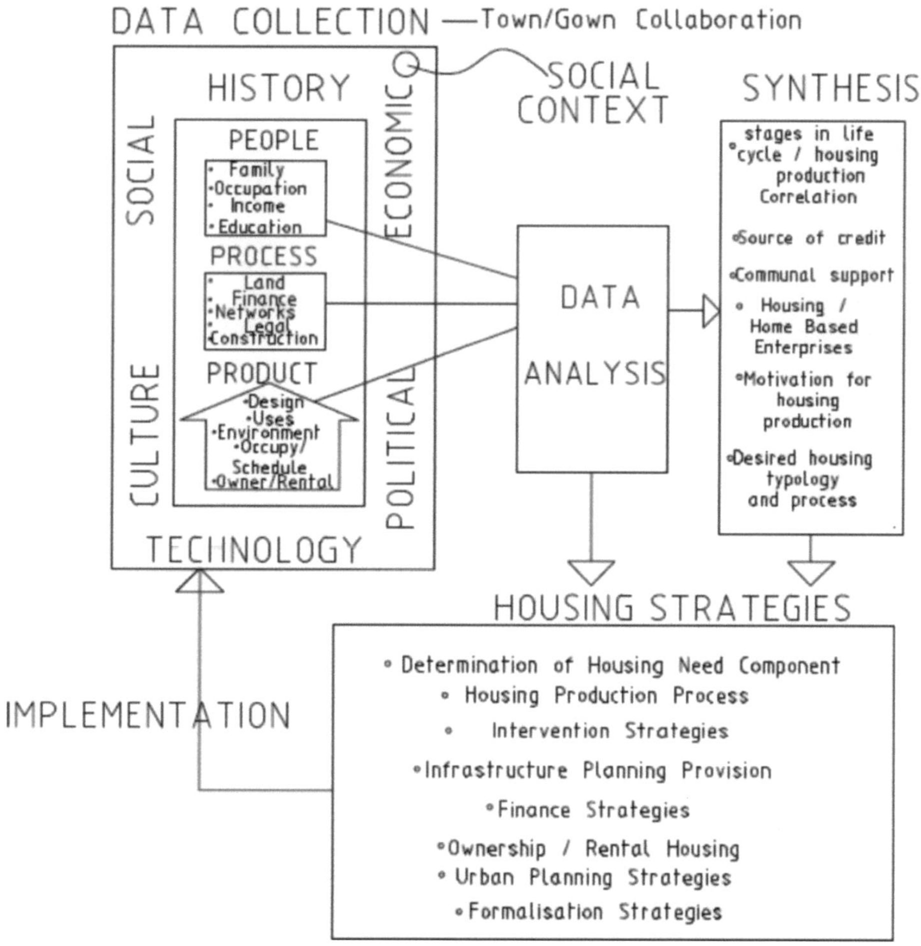

Figure 1.
A cyclic people-centred housing strategy framework.

and families that need housing and their social profile in relation to actions already initiated to actualise housing desire. In the interim, it will be beneficial to do a comprehensive survey of rapidly growing and developing outskirts and suburb of cities. This means working backwards from the field to devising strategies and policies to aid the self-producers of housing and master plan these newly developing areas in ways of reintegrating them to city, regional or national comprehensive plans. In places where the people are building houses on cheap land on the outskirts, government should acquire land for public housing and map out future light industrial areas and other uses like educational, commercial, health and recreational spaces since housing problem is solved individually in these contexts. The resources to execute sites-and-services schemes is rarely available and, if executed, results in over valuing of land beyond the reach of the low income. In practice, cheaper land beyond the sites-and-services scheme is usually the next target of the poor resulting in rapid expansion of low-density cities. Also, the rural and urban areas in these cities are socially interconnected—economically, financially, politically, culturally and technologically. The housing environment on the outskirts has houses belonging to different income groups in an indistinctive way but predominantly to low-income people. Therefore, housing solution should not be seen in isolation of other aspects of development to ensure urban sustainability. Academics and researchers are in a position to bring to the fore negative effects of neoliberal housing processes on the society and policies with class interest through people's perspectives and collaborate with community groups to negotiate better alternative strategies [52].

As shown in **Figure 1**, researchers and public administrators will collaborate in collecting data about family size and composition, occupation, income, education level, residential history and other socio-economic characteristics of the low-income people in rapidly developing outskirts of the city. Data will be collected on the housing process starting from how the land was acquired, the legalisation process, the construction process, who are the actors and participants in the process and how much support they enjoyed from their networks and community. In such informal developments, the houses will be in different stages of completion. The location and environment have to be studied. Data will be collected on the design type of houses, the uses accommodated, the completion and occupying schedule and whether it is occupied by the owner family with or without renters. This list of data needed is not exhaustive depending on the context. These data will be collected simultaneously with information on the history, social, economic, political, cultural and technological situation of the immediate local context and the overall context of the country.

These data will be subjected to univariate, bivariate and multivariate analyses to synthesise information on motivation for housing production, desired housing typologies and process, stages in life cycle and housing production correlation. Other synthesised information will include sources of credit commonly utilised and corresponding modes of collateral security, the communal support the people enjoy including indigenous organisations, the common home-based enterprises, the indigenous or local knowledge in the process and other unexpected information not envisaged that will be useful in formulating housing strategies.

Housing strategies that will emanate from this synthesis will include determination of housing need components, intervention strategies after defining the people that really need housing, what they need, why they need it and their preferred process. Others include finance strategies, urban planning and administration strategies, the meeting and departure points of the informal and formal processes and formalisation strategies that may facilitate equitable housing provision and overall development.

These housing, urban planning and development strategies are implemented and the whole cycle is repeated to review, update, improve and alleviate the housing crisis in these developing countries. Fresh public, private and public-private collaboration housing strategies can evolve independently from better studies and cyclic implementation of this people-centred housing strategy framework after a few cycles in the same location or cycles in different local contexts of the same country.

8. Conclusion

This chapter has highlighted the crisis level of housing shortfall in the developing world, especially concerning low-income people. It took a panoramic view of housing strategies implemented in these countries, evaluated them and pointed to why there is marginal success of internationally backed national housing strategies compared to people's negotiated self-produced housing. The chapter proposes a people-centred approach and a cyclic people-centred housing strategy framework based on the social totality concept of Lefebvre's theory of space. The implementation of the framework needs town and gown collaboration of researchers and professionals in academics, private and public sectors. The cycle starts from collecting data about the people, the process and the houses produced by people and the social, economic, political, cultural and technological characteristics of the immediate local and larger national context. This information is analysed and synthesised to discover people, housing production, housing process, housing uses and typologies, sources of finance, community support, motivation and life cycle correlates. These correlates are critical to deriving housing strategies in defining who needs housing, for what purpose or purposes and when it is needed. It also helps to arrive at appropriate intervention strategies for the process, finance, urban and infrastructure planning and formalisation in ways that will positively affect housing solutions and overall development.

Author details

E. Babatunde Jaiyeoba[1] and Abimbola O. Asojo[2*]

1 Department of Architecture Obafemi Awolowo University, Ile-Ife, Nigeria

2 College of Design, Interior Design, University of Minnesota, Minnesota, USA

*Address all correspondence to: aasojo@umn.edu

References

[1] Hoa JHB. Totality and the common: Henri Lefebvre and Maurice Blanchot on everyday life. Cultural Critique. 2014;**88**(Fall):54-78

[2] Lefebvre H. In: Moore J, editor. Critique of Everyday Life. Vol. 1. New York: Verso; 2008 (orig. pub. 1947 and reissued with a new preface in 1958)

[3] Ram P, Needham B. Why is public policy for affordable housing in India changing so slowly: Explaining institutional inertia. Environment and Urbanization Asia. 2016;7(2):177-195. DOI: 10.1177/0975425316664634

[4] Hananel R, Krefetz SP, Vatury A. Public housing matters: Public housing policy in Sweden, the United States, and Israel. Journal of Planning Education and Research. 2018:1-16. DOI: 10.1177/0739456X18793702

[5] Gough KV, Yankson P. A neglected aspect of the housing market: The caretakers of Peri-urban Accra, Ghana. Urban Studies. 2011;**48**(4):793-810. DOI: 10.1177/0042098010367861

[6] United Nations. World Urbanization Prospects. New York: UN; 2014

[7] United Nations. World Urbanization Prospects, The 2014 Revision, New York and Geneva. 2014. Available from: http://esa.un.org/unpd/wup/cd-rom/ [Accessed: 03 November 2018]

[8] Buckley RM, Kallergis A, Wainer L. Addressing the housing challenge: Avoiding the Ozymandias syndrome. Environment and Urbanization. 2016;**28**:119-138. DOI: 10.1177/0956247815627523

[9] UN-Habitat. Global activities report. Increasing Synergy for greater national ownership. United Nations Human Settlements Programme. 2015:2015

[10] Waeyenberge EV. Crisis? What crisis? A critical appraisal of world bank housing policy in the wake of the global financial crisis. Environment and Planning A: Economy and Space. 2018;**50**(2):288-309. DOI: 10.1177/0308518X17745873

[11] Turner JFC. The squatter settlement: Architecture that works. Architectural Design. 1968;**38**(8):355-360

[12] Turner JFC. Housing priorities, settlement patterns, and urban development in modernizing countries. Journal of the American Institute of Planners. 1968;**34**(6):354-363

[13] Turner JFC. Housing by People: Towards Autonomy in Building Environments. London, UK: Marion Boyars; 1976

[14] De Soto H. The Mystery of Capital. New York: Basic Books; 2000

[15] Sengupta U, Murtagh B, Camila D'Ottaviano C, Pasternak S. Between enabling and provider approach: Key shifts in the national housing policy in India and Brazil. Environment and Planning C: Politics and Space. 2018;**36**(5):856-876. DOI: 10.1177/2399654417725754

[16] UN-Habitat. Enabling Shelter Strategies: Review of Experience from Two Decades of Implementation. UN-Habitat: Nairobi; 2006

[17] UN-Habitat. State of the Worlds Cities. London: Earthscan and UN-HABITAT; 2006

[18] UN-Habitat. World Cities Report. Nairobi: UN Publications; 2016

[19] LIHTC. Compliance Manual. rihousing; March 2013

[20] Land Use Act. Chapter 202, Laws of the Federation of Nigeria. 1990.

Available from: www.nigeria-law.org/Land%20Use%20Act.htm [Retrieved from: 23 July 2019]

[21] Monkkonen P. Transition in Mexico: Expanding access to housing finance. Urban Affairs Review. 2011;**47**(5):672-695. DOI: 10.1177/1078087411400381

[22] Schwartz A. Housing Policy in the United States. 3rd ed. New York: Taylor and Francis, Routledge; 2014

[23] Bloom DD. Learning from New York. Journal of the American Planning Association. 2012;**78**(4):418-431

[24] Hananel R. From central to marginal: The trajectory of Israel's public-housing policy. Urban Studies. 2017;**54**(11):2432-2447. DOI: 10.1177/0042098016649323

[25] Talen E. Zoning and diversity in historical perspective. Journal of Planning History. 2012;**11**(4):330-347

[26] World Bank. Housing: Sector Policy Paper. Washington DC: World Bank; 1975

[27] World bank. Housing: Enabling Markets to Work. World Bank Policy Paper. Washington DC: World Bank; 1993

[28] Wakely P, Riley E. The Case for Incremental Housing. Cities Alliance Policy Research and Working Paper Series. No. 1. Washington DC, USA; 2011

[29] Wakely P. Urban Public Housing Strategies in Developing Countries: Whence and Whither Paradigms, Policies, Programmes and Projects. 2014; DPU60 Working Paper Series: Reflections No. 163/60

[30] Tipple AG, Korboe D, Garrod G, Willis K. Housing supply in Ghana: A study of Accra, Kumasi and Berekum. Progress in Planning. 1999;**51**(4):255-325

[31] Jaiyeoba B. Social Production of Private Low Income Housing in Ogbere, Ibadan. Saarbrucken, Germany: LAP LAMBERT Academic Publishing; 2011

[32] Quigley JM. Just Suppose: Housing Subsidies for Low-Income Renters. Berkeley Program on Housing and Urban Policy Working Paper W06-005. Berkeley: University of California; 2007

[33] Arnott R. Housing Policy in Developing Countries: The Importance of the Informal Economy. Working Paper No. 13. IBRD/World Bank for Commission on Growth and Development. 2008

[34] Gilbert A. The return of the slum: Does language matter. International Journal of Urban and Regional Research. 2007;**31**(4):697-713

[35] Tipple AG. Housing problems and fields for intervention in Ghana. African Urban Studies. 1985;**21**:5-13

[36] Willis KG, Malpezzi S, Tipple G. An econometric and cultural analysis of rent control in Kumasi, Ghana. Urban Studies. 1990;**27**(2):241-258

[37] Konadu-Agyemang K. Structural adjustment programs and housing affordability in Accra, Ghana. The Canadian Geographer. 2001;**45**(4):528-544

[38] Jaiyeoba B, Asojo A. (Re) inventing the (non) role of designers in low-income housing production in the developing world: A case study in Nigeria. The International Journal of Architectonic, Spatial, and Environmental Design. 2015;**9**(3):1-11

[39] Jaiyeoba EB, Asojo AO, Amole B. The Yoruba vernacular as a paradigm for low-income housing: Lessons from Ogbere, Ibadan, Nigeria. Arch Net-International Journal of Architectural Research. 2017;**11**(1):101-118

[40] Federal Government of Nigeria (FGN). National Housing Policy. Nigeria: Federal Ministry of Works and Housing; 2002

[41] Schmidt S, Budinich V. Housing the poor by engaging the private and citizen sectors: Social innovations and 'hybrid value chains'. Global Urban Development Magazine. 2008;**4**(2)

[42] Kellner D. Critical Theory and the Crisis of Social Theory. 1990. Available from: http://www.gseis.ucla.edu/faculty/kellner/kellner.html [Accessed: 27 December 2018]

[43] Arboleda M. Financialization, totality and planetary urbanization in the Chilean Andes. Geoforum. 2015;**67**:4-13. DOI: 10.1016/j.geoforum. [Accessed: 28 December 2018]

[44] Lefebvre H. In: Moore J, editor. Critique of Everyday Life. Vol. 2. Foundations for a Sociology of the Everyday. New York: Verso; 2008 (orig. pub. 1961)

[45] Lefebvre H. Le Droit à la Ville. The Right to the City. 2nd ed. Paris, France: Anthropos; 1968

[46] Bower R. Who decides and who provides? The anarchistic housing practices of John Turner as realizations of Henri Lefebvre's Autogestive space. Alternatives: Global, Local, Political. 2016;**41**(2):83-97

[47] Lefebvre H. Rhythmanalysis: Space, Time and Everyday Life. London: Continuum; 2004.p 169

[48] Giddens A. Sociology. A Brief but Critical Introduction. 2nd ed. London: MacMillan Press; 1986

[49] Butler C. Law and the social production of space [Ph.D thesis]. Queensland: Griffith University; 2003

[50] Jaiyeoba B, Aklanoglu F. Theory of social production and socio-economic issues in low income housing in Ogbere, Ibadan. Journal of ASIAN Behavioural Studies. 2018;**3**(7):121-130. DOI: 10.21834/jabs.v3i7.264

[51] Stephens M. Locating Chinese urban housing policy in an international context. Urban Studies. 2010;**47**(14):2965-2982. DOI: 10.1177/0042098009360219

[52] Hodkinson S, Watt P, Mooney G. Introduction: Neoliberal housing policy—Time for a critical re-appraisal. Critical Social Policy. 2012;**33**(1):3-16. DOI: 10.1177/0261018312457862

Chapter 2

Temporal MCDA Methods for Decision-Making in Sustainable Development Context

Anissa Frini, Sarah Benamor and Bruno Urli

Abstract

Public decision-making problems are more and more complex in a context where decisions have to be made based concurrently on economic, social, and environmental considerations. In this context, decisions need to be evaluated in the short, medium, and long term because their planning horizons are usually of several years or even decades. A literature review on MCDA methods used in the sustainable development (SD) context shows that most MCDA methods used are static and existing research does not propose any aggregation framework for temporal assessment of actions. In the last 5 years, development of temporal MCDA has witnessed the interest of some researchers. However, the latest developments remain limited, and only a few research studies offer aggregation frameworks for multi-period settings. This paper presents two recent temporal MCDA methods that were applied in SD context. The first is MUPOM method which demonstrates how outranking methods, based on concordance-discordance principles, can be generalized to processing temporal impacts of decisions. The second, named PROMETHEE-MP, consists of a multi-period generalization of PROMETHEE under random uncertainty.

Keywords: multi-criteria decision aid (MCDA), multi-period evaluations, outranking methods, sustainable development, PROMETHEE, MUPOM

1. Introduction

Decision-making processes today evolve in a context where sustainability is an important issue. Decisions have to be made while concurrently evaluating their economic, social, and environmental consequences. The most quoted definition of sustainable development (SD) is that of the report of Brundtland Commission [1] entitled "Our Common Future," where sustainable development is defined as "development that meets the needs of the present without compromising the ability of future generations to meet their own needs. This definition contains two key concepts: (i) the concept of needs, in particular the essential needs of the world's poor, to which overriding priority should be given; and (ii) the idea of limitations imposed by the state of technology and social organization on the environment's ability to meet present and future needs." This definition indicates the three main pillars of sustainable development, i.e., economic growth, environmental protection, and social equality. Secondly, it puts emphases on the long-term vision associated with sustainable development. In fact, decision processes should take into account not only the immediate but also the future consequences of decisions in order not to compromise future generations. In such context, decisions are generally ill-defined, the impacts of decisions are uncertain and often difficult to measure, and the acceptability of decisions is more difficult to attain. And so, the need for using structured methods and novel approaches to support sustainable decisions has emerged.

A state-of-the-art survey on sustainable decision prioritization [2] shows multi-criteria decision aid (MCDA) methods are the most popular approach to support sustainable decisions. These methods enable the simultaneous consideration of conflicting criteria as it occurs in a real-world problem under sustainability imperatives. However, although sustainable development tries to reach a balance between the evaluations of actions in the short and the long term, most articles surveyed in [2] did not investigate the long-term perspective related to sustainable development. Only very recently have some researchers proposed novel temporal MCDA methods for application in SD context. But, the state of the art remains limited, and only a few research studies offer temporal aggregation frameworks.

This paper presents two novel temporal MCDA methods that were applied in SD context. The first is MUPOM method (MUlti-criteria multi-Period Outranking Method) which demonstrates how outranking methods can be used in processing the temporal impacts of decisions. The second method is named PROMETHEE-MP and consists of a temporal generalization of PROMETHEE in a context of random uncertainty. This paper is organized as follows: Section 2 presents the previous work. Section 3 proposes a formulation for decision-making problem in SD context. Sections 4 and 5 expose the MUPOM and PROMETHEE-MP methods. Section 6 provides an illustration of these two methods on the same case study. Finally, Section 7 concludes the paper.

2. Previous work

Despite the importance of temporal (multi-periods) evaluation of actions for sustainable decisions, only a few articles have dealt with this aspect. Some authors consider the long-term effects as a criterion [3, 4], while others use scenario planning and predictive techniques or fuzzy modeling to deal with future unknowns [5]. In [6], the long-term effects are discounted, and in [4] they are roughly and qualitatively assessed. Very recently, some temporal extensions of MCDA methods have been developed [3, 6, 7–11]. In a forest management context, the long-term impacts were addressed as a specific criterion [3], and the local community was asked to evaluate it. In [6], the authors proposed a sustainable environmental management system (SEMS) where actions are ranked using ELECTRE III. The authors indicate that special care was taken in the assessment of criteria and that expected short- and long-term consequences were considered but without any explanation on how this was achieved. In [9], a multi-period multi-criteria method based on adapting TOPSIS to temporal context is proposed. But, compensation between the decision criteria on which TOPSIS rely (as scoring methods) is not appropriate for sustainability. In [10], authors generalize PROMETHEE to temporal setting. The weighted mean is applied for aggregation of the net flow scores over the periods, and then the method is compensatory. Another PROMETHEE-based model was published in [11] to assess the long-term impact of energy supply technologies. In this research work, different criteria weights were considered depending on the life cycle steps (from introduction to saturation of the market).

The literature review presented here shows a limited state of the art and an as yet largely undeveloped research area on multi-period aggregation. As discussed earlier, compensation is the main issue behind the few existing temporal proposals.

We believe outranking methods are more suitable for sustainable decision problems because of their level of compensation (partial or non-compensatory), their use of thresholds, and their use of different types of data/criteria (qualitative and quantitative) without the need for normalization. To the best of our knowledge, research on developing temporal **outranking** methods is not well advanced. In this context, we started a research program to develop temporal outranking MCDA methods. In 2019, our research team proposed a generalization of outranking methods to temporal context and show how they can be applied for processing temporal impacts of decisions [7, 8]. Frini and Benamor [7] propose the first outranking method for multi-period (temporal) evaluations of actions called MUPOM. Based on pairwise comparisons, outranking relations and a measure of distance between preference relations, MUPOM accommodates the requirements of sustainable development discussed earlier and supports decisions that comply with the long-term vision related to SD context. Besides, existing research works dealing with MCDA methods under uncertainty are developed for static MCDA methods [12–18]. In order to develop extend MCDA under uncertainty to temporal context, we proposed in [8] a temporal generalization of PROMETHEE in a context of uncertainty. In the rest of the present paper, two generalizations of the outranking methods MUPOM and PROMETHEE-MP are presented and the results of their application on the same case study compared. The next sections expose the main results of this research program.

3. Problem formulation

In order to formulate the problem, let us consider a set A of N candidate actions $(a_1, \ldots a_N)$, a set T of K assessment periods $(P_1, \ldots, P_K)$, a set C of M criteria $(C_1, C_2 \ldots, C_M)$, a set Π of M criteria weights $(\pi_1, \ldots \pi_M)$, *a set* $(\alpha_1, \ldots, \alpha_K)$ of the K relative importance of periods $(P_1, \ldots, P_K)$, and $g_j(a_i)$ the evaluation of an action a_i on criterion j.

The following assumptions of the model are made. (i) All evaluations are evaluated in the future with no missing evaluations. (ii) Criteria weights may change over time. (iii) Criteria, preference functions, and thresholds can vary over time. (iv) Criteria $(C_1, C_2 \ldots, C_M)$ are assumed to be independent.

Figure 1 displays the decision matrices for multi-period multi-criteria decision problems.

4. MUPOM: multi-criteria multi-period outranking method

MUPOM (MUlti-criteria multi-Period Outranking Method) is a three-phase temporal outranking MCDA method. In Phase 1, multi-criteria aggregation is performed in order to obtain outranking and preference relations for each period

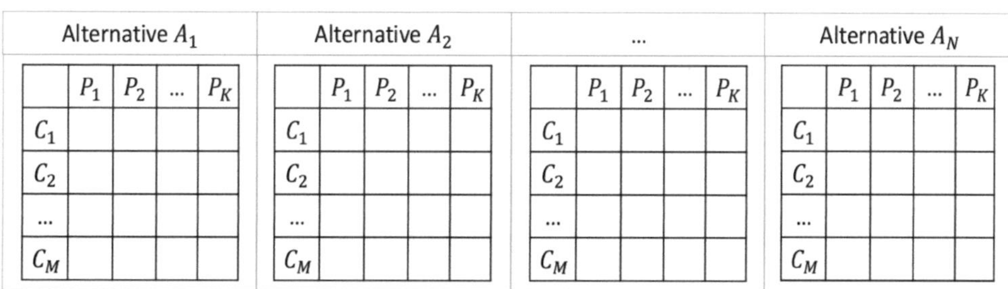

Figure 1.
Decision matrices for the considered decision problems.

and for each pair of actions. Then in Phase 2 and for each pair of actions, a measure of distance between preference relations is used for temporal aggregation of the preference relations obtained in Phase 1. A graph showing relations between all pairs of actions illustrates the results of this aggregation. Next, in Phase 3 an exploitation procedure is used to compute the performance of each action a_i. The following subsections provide details on the three phases. A full version of the mathematical details of the method is provided in [7].

Figure 2 graphs the steps of the MUPOM method.

4.1 Phase 1: multi-criteria aggregation

Multi-criteria aggregation relies on pairwise comparisons and concordance-discordance principles. For each pair of actions, we compute the concordance index (resp. discordance index), which evaluates the extent to which the criterion agrees (does not agree) with the assertion "action a_i is at-least as good as action a_k." Then, if a majority of the criteria support this assertion and if the opposition of the other criteria—the minority—is not "too strong," action a_i is declared to be at least as good as action a_k. Strong and weak outranking relations are constructed at this step. Next, the obtained outranking relations are transformed into preference relations $(P, Q, I, R, Q^{-1}, P^{-1})$. Thus, for each pair of actions and for each period, we obtain either a strict preference (P), weak preference (Q), indifference (I), incomparability (R), inverse weak preference (Q^{-1}), or inverse strict preference (P^{-1}). The multi-criteria aggregation is a four-step phase [7]:

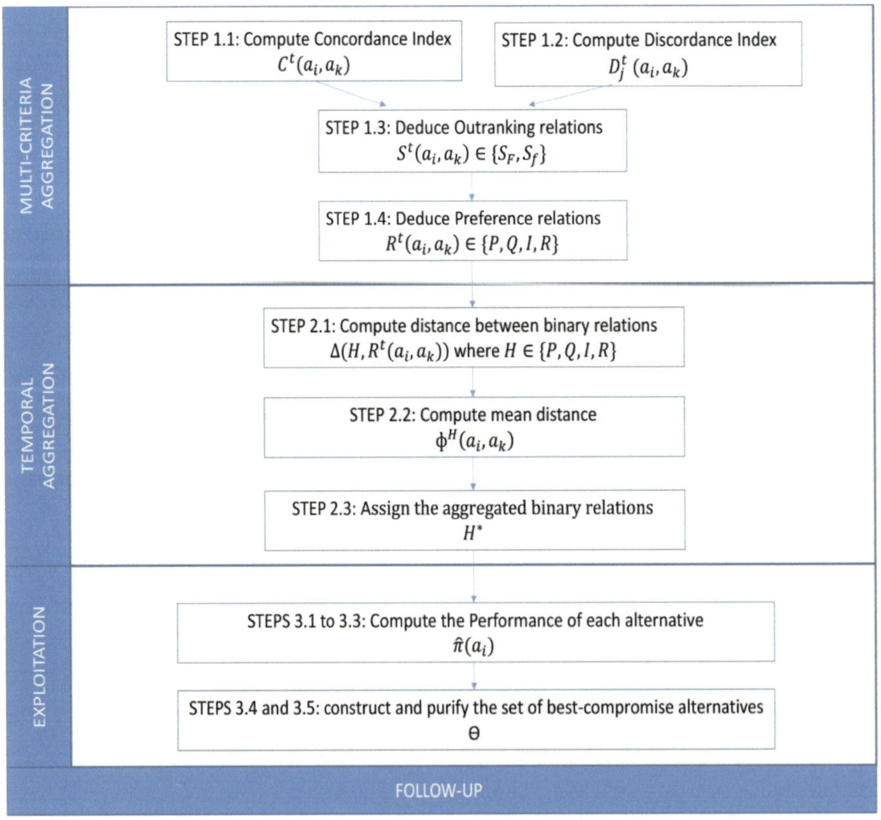

Figure 2.
Steps of the MUPOM method [7].

Step 1.1: For each period t and for each pair of actions(a_i, a_k), compute the concordance index $C^t(a_i, a_k)$.

Step 1.2: For each period t, for each pair of actions (a_i, a_k), and for each criterion j, compute the discordance index $D_j^t(a_i, a_k)$.

Step 1.3: Construct the relational preference systems $S^t(a_i, a_k)$ for each pair of actions (a_i, a_k) and for each period t using concordance and discordance thresholds. We deduce that action a_i strongly outranks a_k $(a_i S_F a_k)$ or a_i weakly outranks $a_k (a_i S_f a_k)$.

Step 1.4: For each period t and for each pair of actions (a_i, a_k), convert the obtained outranking relations to preference relation $R^t(a_i, a_k) \in (P, Q, I, R, Q^{-1}, P^{-1})$ where P, Q, I, R refers, respectively, to strict preference, weak preference, indifference, and incomparability. We note $a_i P^{-1} a_k$ for $a_k P a_i$, and $a_i Q^{-1} a_k$ for $a_k Q a_i$.

4.2 Phase 2: temporal aggregation

This phase consists of aggregating the preference relations obtained for each pair of actions and at each period (results of Phase 1). This aggregation is done using a measure of distance between preorders [19]. Thus, the aggregated preference relation which minimizes the distance with the preorders at each period is obtained. The temporal aggregation phase consists of three steps [7]:

Step 2.1: For each pair of actions (a_i, a_k) and at each period t, compute the distance between the preference relation $R^t(a_i, a_k)$ resulting from Step 1.4 and each possible preference relation $H \in (P, Q, I, R, Q^{-1}, P^{-1})$. This distance is noted $\Delta(H, R^t(a_i, a_k))$.

Step 2.2: Aggregate the distances obtained at each period into a mean distance $\Phi^H(a_i, a_k)$.$\Phi^H(a_i, a_k) = \sum_{t=1}^{T} \alpha_t \Delta(H, R_t(a_i, a_k))$ where α_t is the relative importance of period t.

Step 2.3: Assign to the pair of actions(a_i, a_k) the preference relation H^*, such as:

$$H^* = \left\{H^* / \Phi^{H^*} = min_{H \in (P,Q,I,R,Q^{-1},P^{-1})} \Phi^H(a_i, a_k)\right\}$$

A graph representing relations between all pairs of actions displays the results.

4.3 Phase 3: exploitation

This phase consists of computing the performance of each action a_i . Performance calculation is based on the number of actions that are preferred (strictly or weakly) to a_i and those that a_i are preferred to (strictly or weakly). The set of "best compromise" action(s) is then deduced based on the computed performance. This set contains the actions with the highest performance and those which are incomparable to them. Details on the exploitation phase are provided in [19].

MUPOM method has important contributions. First, it proposes a generalization of outranking methods based on ELECTRE principles (concordance, discordance, and credibility indexes) to multi-period and temporal settings. Consequently, the method supports partial preferences and partial rankings and confirms that the outranking methods can be generalized to temporal context. In practical terms, MUPOM provides valuable contributions for researchers and practitioners concerned with decision-making processes under sustainability. Beyond the financial dimension, it enables integration of social and environmental impacts in the short, medium, and long term. By taking into account immediate and future consequences of actions, it guarantees decisions are not made that compromise future generations.

5. PROMETHEE-MP: a generalization of PROMETHEE for multi-period evaluations under uncertainty

PROMETHEE-MP is a recently developed temporal outranking method that allows aggregation of multi-periods and uncertain evaluations. It consists of three phases. Phase 1 aggregates the criteria, at each period of the horizon, based on PROMETHEE outgoing and incoming flows and Monte Carlo simulations. Binary relations are computed for each pair of actions. Phase 2 consists of aggregating the binary relations obtained over the periods using the measure of distance between preorders [19] as is done with MUPOM. Finally, in Phase 3 the performance of each action a_i is computed, based on the number of actions that are preferred (strictly or weakly) to a_i and those that a_i are preferred to (strictly or weakly). **Figure 2** presents all the steps of PROMETHEE-MP. The following subsections provide details on the three phases. A full version of the mathematical details of the method is found in [8] (**Figure 3**).

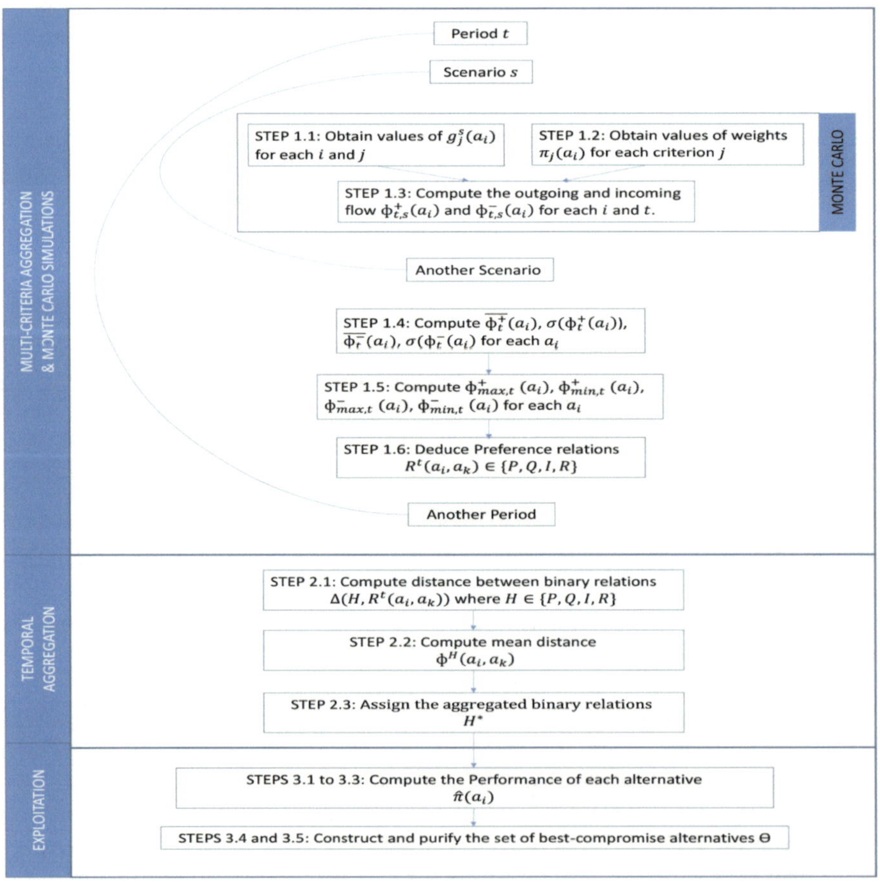

Figure 3.
Steps of PROMETHEE-MP [8].

5.1 Phase 1: multi-criteria aggregation and Monte Carlo simulations

In Phase 1, the criteria at each period of the horizon are aggregated. The method looks at a representation of uncertainty with probability distributions for uncertain parameters (evaluations and weights) and uses Monte Carlo simulation to generate numerical values for each uncertainty scenario. In this illustration and without loss of generality, uniform distributions using intervals are simulated for each parameter and for each period t. For each scenario of uncertainty s, we generate from the interval a specific value for evaluations and weights. Then at each period t and for each scenario$s$, we use the PROMETHEE method, and we compute outgoing $\varnothing_{t,s}^{+}(a_i)$ and incoming flows $\varnothing_{t,s}^{-}(a_i)$ for each action a_i. As part of the model, we propose a generalization of PROMETHEE III that associates an interval to the outgoing and incoming flows for each action and deduces a partial preorder for the actions. The multi-criteria aggregation and Monte Carlo simulation phase consists of these steps [8]:

Steps 1.1 and 1.2: For each period t, we conduct a Monte Carlo simulation s. Each simulation generates, for each criterion j, a specific evaluation of action a_i noted $g_j^{t,s}(a_i)$ in the interval $[g_j^{-}(a_i), g_j^{+}(a_i)]$. Also, each simulation considers a different value for criteria weights for each criterion j, noted $\pi_j^{t,s}(a_i)$.

Step 1.3: For each scenario$s$, action i and period t, we apply PROMETHEE and compute outgoing and incoming flows $\varnothing_{t,s}^{+}(a_i)$ and $\varnothing_{t,s}^{-}(a_i)$.

Step 1.4: In this step, the outgoing and incoming flow distributions are defined by computing the mean $\overline{\varnothing_t^{+}}(a_i)$and $\overline{\varnothing_t^{-}}(a_i)$ and the standard deviations $\sigma\left(\varnothing_t^{+}(a_i)\right)$ and $\sigma\left(\varnothing_t^{-}(a_i)\right)$.

Step 1.5: The resulting interval limits of the outgoing and incoming flows$\varnothing_{max,t}^{+}(a_i)$, $\varnothing_{min,t}^{+}(a_i)$, $\varnothing_{max,t}^{-}(a_i)$, $\varnothing_{min,t}^{-}(a_i)$ are deduced.

Step 1.6: Preference relations $S_t(a_i, a_k)\epsilon\{I, P, Q, R\}$ are deduced, depending on the values of $\varnothing_{max,t}^{+}(a_i)$, $\varnothing_{min,t}^{+}(a_i)$, $\varnothing_{max,t}^{-}(a_i)$, $\varnothing_{min,t}^{-}(a_i)$ (see [8]).

5.2 Phase 2: temporal aggregation

Here the temporal aggregation procedure of MUPOM (Section 4.2) is used to aggregate the preference relations obtained over the periods in Step 1.6. As with the MUPOM method, the measure of distance between preorders developed in [19] is used.

5.3 Phase 3: exploitation

The temporal exploitation procedure of MUPOM (Section 4.3) is used in this phase. It computes the performance of each action a_i based on the number of actions that are preferred (strictly or weakly) to a_i and those that a_i are preferred to (strictly or weakly).

6. Case study

In this section, MUPOM and PROMETHEE-MP are applied in the context of sustainable forest management. Sustainable forest management is a well-suited application context since it considers conflicting and heterogeneous criteria that should be assessed on about 150 years ahead. Actually, the selection of sustainable forest management options should arrive at a balance between biodiversity, soil and water conservation, forest productivity, socioeconomic benefits, and the population's values and needs. Second, the impact of each decision has to be assessed long term over the period of forest regeneration (about 150 years).

Five options are for consideration: (a_1) a reference option corresponding to the terms of the intervention standards regulation; (a_2) a removal of protected areas for wood production; (a_3) a specific plan for protecting the caribou habitat; (a_4) a reforestation program; and (a_5) a variable-level harvesting strategy which accelerates the harvest rate for the near periods. For evaluating these forest management options, we consider five criteria assessed every 5 years: (C_1) the 5-year exploitable volume, (C_2) index of caribou habitat, (C_3) good habitat for moose, (C_4) old forest areas, and (C_5) carbon footprint. **Figure 4** provides an example of the evolution over time (30 periods of 5 years) of criteria C_2.

The AHP method was used to model the preferences in terms of criteria weights. A questionnaire was presented to an expert asking for pairwise comparisons between pairs of criteria and for the indifference, preference, and veto thresholds for each criterion, as well as the most appropriate criteria functions to be used with PROMETHEE. Also requested was the relative importance of periods. **Tables 1–3** present the weights and an overview of the data used for option a_3, respectively. Used weights and data for MUPOM are crisp and for PROMETHEE-MP are intervals.

To start, Phase 1 of MUPOM and PROMETHEE-MP is applied. Results are obtained in terms of binary relations (P, Q, I, R, Q^{-1}, P^{-1}) for each pair of actions

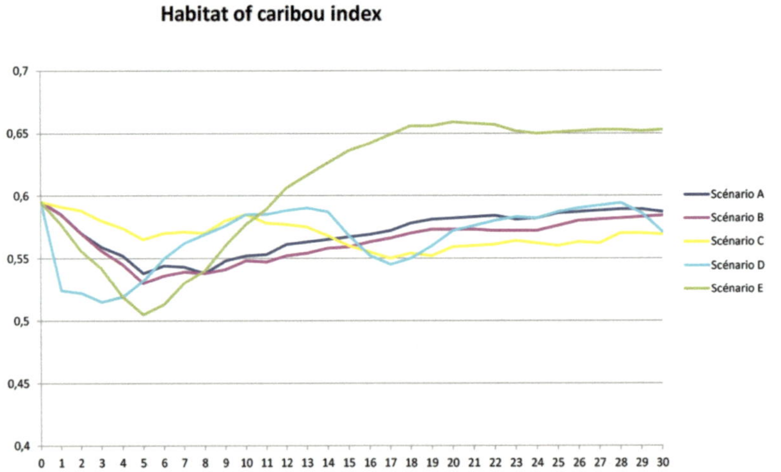

Figure 4.
Evolution over time of the criteria.

	Criteria	Crisp weights for MUPOM	Weights intervals for PROMETHEE-MP
C1	5-year exploitable volume	0.1443	[0.137, 0.151]
C2	Index of caribou habitat	0.3064	[0.291, 0.322]
C3	Good habitat for moose	0.1606	[0.153, 0.169]
C4	Old forest areas	0.3063	[0.291, 0.322]
C5	Carbon footprint	0.0825	[0.078, 0.087]

Table 1.
Criteria weight intervals.

Period	C1 (millions of m^3)	C2 (in [0, 1])	C3 (thousands of hectares)	C4 (thousands of hectares)	C5 (tons of CO2)
P1	39	0.591	295	361	143,716,919
P2	36	0.588	297	362	145,123,580
…	…	…	…	…	…
…	…	…	…	…	…
P30	19	0.569	453	262	225,395,456

Table 2.
Decision matrix for option C used with MUPOM.

Period	C1 (millions of m^3)	C2 (in [0, 1])	C3 (thousands of hectares)	C4 (thousands of hectares)	C5 (tons of CO2)
P1	[37.05, 40.95]	[0.561, 0.620]	[280.25, 309.75]	[342.95, 379.05]	[136,531,073; 150,902,765]
P2	[34.20, 37.80]	[0.558, 0.617]	[282.15, 311.85]	[343.90, 380.10]	[137,867,401; 152,379,759]
…	…	…	…	…	…
…	…	…	…	…	…
P30	[18.05, 19.05]	[0.540, 0.597]	[430.35, 475.65]	[248.9, 275.1]	[214,125,683; 236,665,229]

Table 3.
Decision matrix for option C used with PROMETHEE-MP.

and for each period. **Table 4** shows the results of Phase 1 of MUPOM and PROMETHEE-MP for the pair (a_1, a_2). Then, in Phase 2, the results for each period are aggregated using the temporal aggregation procedure. For each pair of actions, **Table 5** shows the aggregated relation which minimizes the distance between the relations obtained at each period and the set of preference relations (P, Q, I, P-1, Q-1).

A graph representing relations between all pairs of actions illustrates the results. Phase 3 consists of exploiting the graph (**Figures 5** and **6**) and determining which action performs better. Results of MUPOM show $\{a_2, a_5\}$ are the best compromise solutions, whereas PROMETHEE-MP shows $\{a_5\}$ as the only best compromise solution.

Results show that in a deterministic context and without considering uncertainty, the two options a_2 and a_5 are both of best compromise and incomparable. However, when considering uncertainty on the evaluations and weights, only a_5 is then of best compromise. It should first be noted that by modeling uncertainty on the evaluation and weights, as done with PROMETHEE-MP, the result is more robust because it takes into account the variability of evaluation over the intervals. However, comparison of results given by the two methods needs to take into account that they are not based on the same foundations. MUPOM uses concordance-discordance principles as ELECTRE methods do, while PROMETHEE-MP uses outgoing and incoming flows as PROMETHHE methods do.

In future research, it will be important to validate the findings of the two models by comparing the obtained results with those given by a panel of expert in forest management. A Delphi procedure could be applied in order to get the opinion of experts on the results. A level of 70% of agreement between experts will be considered. This validation process will confirm the quality of the results given by the method.

Period	Preference relation resulting from MUPOM	Preference relation resulting from PROMETHEE-MP	Period	Preference relation resulting from MUPOM	Preference relation resulting from PROMETHEE-MP
1	P-1	P-1	16	R	P-1
2	P-1	P-1	17	Q-1	P-1
3	Q	P-1	18	Q-1	P-1
4	Q	P-1	19	Q-1	P-1
5	P	Q-1	20	Q-1	Q-1
6	P	I	21	Q-1	Q-1
7	P	I	22	Q-1	Q-1
8	R	I	23	Q-1	I
9	R	Q-1	24	Q-1	I
10	Q	Q-1	25	Q-1	I
11	R	P	26	Q-1	P-1
12	R	R	27	Q-1	P-1
13	Q	Q	28	Q-1	P-1
14	Q	R	29	Q-1	I
15	R	Q-1	30	Q-1	P-1

Table 4.
Preference relations resulting from multi-criteria aggregation for pair (a_1, a_2).

Pair	Aggregated relation with MUPOM	Aggregated relation with PROMETHEE-MP	Pair	Aggregated relation with MUPOM	Aggregated relation with PROMETHEE-MP
(a_1, a_2)	Q-1	P-1	(a_2, a_4)	R	P
(a_2, a_1)	Q	P	(a_4, a_2)	R	P-1
(a_1, a_3)	P	P	(a_2, a_5)	R	P-1
(a_3, a_1)	P-1	P-1	(a_5, a_2)	R	P
(a_1, a_4)	R	Q-1	(a_3, a_4)	Q-1	P-1
(a_4, a_1)	R	Q	(a_4, a_3)	Q	P
(a_1, a_5)	R	P-1	(a_3, a_5)	R	P-1
(a_5, a_1)	R	P	(a_5, a_3)	R	P
(a_2, a_3)	Q	P	(a_4, a_5)	R	P-1
(a_3, a_2)	Q-1	P-1	(a_5, a_4)	R	P

Table 5.
Preference relations resulting from temporal aggregation for each pair of actions.

Besides, for stronger interpretation of results, future work will focus on applying the proposed methods on different horizons. For instance, in our case study, we can apply MUPOM and PROMETHEE-MP on the short-term horizon (aggregation of evaluations of the first 20 years), the medium term (aggregation of evaluations of year 20 to year 50), and finally the long term (aggregation of evaluations of year 50 to year 150). By doing so, we can compare the different results depending on the

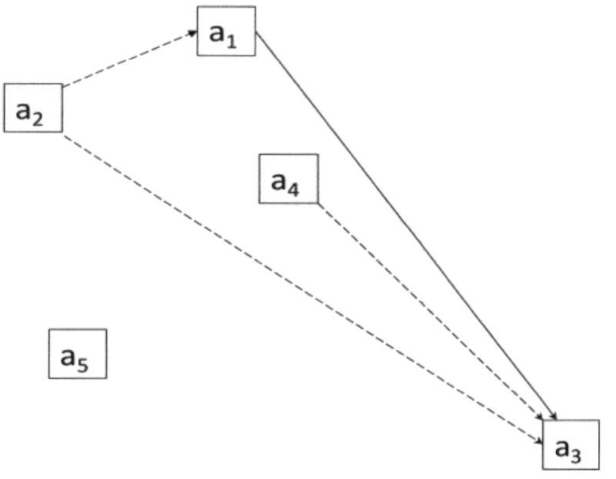

Figure 5.
Exploitation graph with MUPOM.

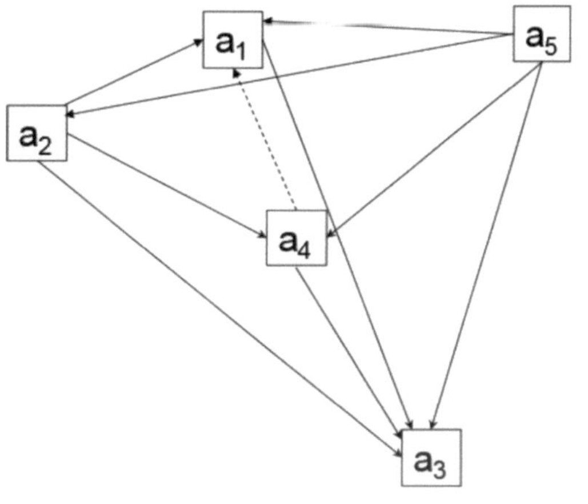

Figure 6.
Exploitation graph with PROMETHEE-MP.

horizon and limit the effect of the aggregation. Results will show if the best compromised option on the whole horizon will differ or not from to the best compromised options in the short, medium, and long term.

7. Conclusion

This paper presents the main results of a recent research program on developing temporal outranking MCDA methods. It presents two generalizations of outranking methods to temporal context to show how outranking methods can be of use in processing the temporal impacts of decisions. The state of the art in this research area still remains limited, and such a proposal is valuable to support sustainable decision-making processes. This paper exposes two recent temporal outranking methods and displays the results of their application in SD context. The MUPOM method demonstrates how outranking methods and, more specifically, the ELECTRE concordance-discordance principles can be of use in processing temporal impacts of decisions. PROMETHEE-MP consists of a multi-period generalization of PROMETHEE under random uncertainty using Monte Carlo simulations. Their application on the same case study shows their applicability.

Funding

This research was funded by "Fonds de recherche du Québec – Societé et Culture."

Author details

Anissa Frini[1]*, Sarah Benamor[2] and Bruno Urli[1]

1 University of Québec at Rimouski, Lévis, Canada

2 University of Ottawa, Ottawa, Canada

*Address all correspondence to: anissa_frini@uqar.ca

References

[1] Brundtland GH. Report of the World Commission on Environment and Development: Our Common Future. Oxford: Oxford University Press; 1987

[2] Kandakoglu A, Frini A, Benamor S. Multi-criteria decision making for sustainable development: A systematic review. Journal of Multi-Criteria Decision Analysis. 2019;**26**:202-251

[3] Balana BB, Mathijs E, Muys B. Assessing the sustainability of forest management: An application of multi-criteria decision analysis to community forests in northern Ethiopia. Journal of Environmental Management. 2010;**91**: 1294-1304. DOI: 10.1016/j.jenvman.2010.02.005

[4] Betrie GD, Sadiq R, Morin KA, Tesfamariam S. Selection of remedial alternatives for mine sites: A multicriteria decision analysis approach. Journal of Environmental Management. 2013;**119**:36-46. DOI: 10.1016/j.jenvman.2013.01.024

[5] Scholten L, Schuwirth N, Reichert P, Lienert J. Tackling uncertainty in multi-criteria decision analysis – An application to water supply infrastructure planning. European Journal of Operational Research. 2015; **242**:243-260. DOI: 10.1016/j.ejor.2014.09.044

[6] Khalili NR, Duecker S. Application of multi-criteria decision analysis in design of sustainable environmental management system framework. Journal of Cleaner Production. 2013;**47**: 188-198. DOI: 10.1016/j.jclepro.2012.10.044

[7] Frini A, Benamor S. MUPOM: A multi-criteria multi-period outranking method for decision-making in sustainable development context. Environmental Impact Assessment Review. 2019;**76**:10-25. DOI: 10.1016/j.eiar.2018.11.002

[8] Urli B, Frini A, Benamor S. PROMETHEE-MP: A generalization of PROMETHEE for multi-period evaluations under uncertainty. International Journal of Multi-Criteria Decision Making. 2019;**8**(1):13-37. DOI: 10.1504/IJMCDM.2019.10019420

[9] Frini A, Benamor S. Making decisions in a sustainable development context: A state-of-the-art survey and proposal of a multi-period single synthesizing criterion approach. Computational Economics. 2017;**52**(2):341-385. DOI: 10.1007/s10614-017-9677-5

[10] Benamar I, De Smet Y. An extension of PROMETHEE II to temporal evaluations. International Journal of Multi-criteria Decision Making. 2018; **3-4**:7. DOI: 10.1504/IJMCDM.2018.094371

[11] Oberschmidt J, Geldermann J, Ludwig J, Schmehl M. Modified PROMETHEE approach for assessing energy technologies. International Journal of Energy Sector Management. 2010;**4**:183-212. DOI: 10.1108/17506221080000394

[12] Corrente S, Figueira JR, Greco S. The SMAA-PROMETHEE method. European Journal of Operational Research. 2014;**239**(2):514-522. DOI: 10.1016/j.ejor.2014.05.026

[13] Khalili-Damghani K, sadi-Nezhad S. A hybrid fuzzy multiple criteria group decision making approach for sustainable project selection. Applied Soft Computing. 2013a;**13**:339-352. DOI: 10.1016/j.asoc.2012.07.030

[14] Khalili-Damghani K, sadi-Nezhad S. A decision support system for fuzzy multi-objective multi-period sustainable project selection. Computers and

Industrial Engineering. 2013b;**64**: 1045-1060. DOI: 10.1016/j.cie.2013.01.016

[15] Baudry G, Macharis C, Vallée T. Range-based multi-actor multi-criteria analysis: A combined method of multi-actor multi-criteria analysis and Monte Carlo simulation to support participatory decision making under uncertainty. European Journal of Operational Research. 2018;**264**(1): 257-269. DOI: 10.1016/j.ejor.2017.06.036

[16] Van Der Kleij C, Hulscher S, Louters T. Comparing uncertain alternatives for a possible airport island location in the North Sea. Ocean and Coastal Management. 2003;**46**: 1031-1047. DOI: 10.1016/j.ocecoaman.2003.09.001

[17] Mirakyan A, De Guio R. Modelling and uncertainties in integrated energy planning. Renewable and Sustainable Energy Reviews. 2015;**46**:62-69. DOI: 10.1016/j.rser.2015.02.028

[18] Ascough JC, Maier HR, Ravalico JK, Strudley MW. Future research challenges for incorporation of uncertainty in environmental and ecological decision-making. Ecological Modelling. 2008;**219**:383-399. DOI: 10.1016/j.ecolmodel.2008.07.015

[19] Benamor S, Martel J-M. A new distance measure including the weak preference relation: Application to the multiple criteria aggregation procedure for mixed evaluation. European Journal of Operational Research. 2014;**237**: 1165-1169. DOI: 10.1016/j.ejor.2014.03.036

Chapter 3

Integrating Water-Food-Energy Nexus with Climate Services: Modelling and Assessment for a Case Study in Africa

Phoebe Koundouri and Lydia Papadaki

Abstract

This chapter is based on the work of DAFNE project, a decision analytic framework to explore the water-energy-food (WEF) nexus in complex transboundary water resources of fast developing countries. In particular, we developed three geo- and temporally referenced scenarios under economic growth and climate change in the Zambezi river basin (ZRB), which is the fourth largest river basin in Africa and located in eight different countries.[1] The future scenarios are conceptually driven by the selected combination of the shared socio-economic pathways (SSPs) and the Representative Concentration Pathway (RCP) 4.5. The time horizon of the explored case study in the ZRB shared by eight countries is the period from 2018 to 2060. The aim of this work is to develop a better understanding of the WEF nexus by providing the input to a cost-benefit optimization model aiming to optimally allocate over time and space water-energy-food. The findings show that the water, energy and food requirements are expected to double during the period of interest considering only demographic development, while economic development and international trade will put an additional burden to the supply chain in meeting those goals.

Keywords: modelling tool, integrated assessment, river basin, demographic index, water, electricity and food projections, economic indexes forecast, nexus, Africa

1. Introduction

Developing countries are in front of unprecedented changes, which will determine their paths in economic, environmental and social terms. Climate change, demographic explosion, new international strategies and economic development opportunities constitute some of the competitive drivers of their future pathways.

The Zambezi river basin (ZRB) is the fourth largest basin of Africa with an area of 1.32 million km^2 shared by eight countries (Angola, Botswana, Malawi, Mozambique, Namibia, Tanzania, Zambia and Zimbabwe) and populated by almost 40 million inhabitants. Currently, the available resource meets the water requirements in the Zambezi basin as a whole. However, possible conflicts between

---

[1] Zambia, Angola, Zimbabwe, Mozambique, Malawi, Botswana, Tanzania, Namibia.

riparian countries in the ZRB can arise due to the asymmetry between resource availability and population density in addition to the fact that the riparian countries have different river basin shares and investment potential, thus determining a different capability to access and use the available resource.

The first section of this chapter will present the storyline and the assumptions of each of the three future scenarios derived by the integration of the representative concentration pathways (RCPs) into the shared socio-economic pathways (SSPs).

The second and third sections deal with the demographic explosion of the riparian countries as a whole and specifically within the Zambezi area and its implication in future water-energy-food consumption.

The last section presents the economic plans of each riparian country in alignment with their long-term Gross Domestic Value (GDP) growth estimations and how the GDP composition projections impact the water and energy requirements of each economic sector. Lastly, a comparative summary of all scenarios is presented leading to the main conclusions of this chapter.

2. Development of the SSPs

This chapter presents socio-economic scenarios comprised of two core elements: a storyline and the table of descriptors. The scenarios refer to a qualitative narrative describing a potential future in combination with quantitative socio-economic elements and trends. The research adopts the SSPs developed by Kriegler [1]. All of them consider mitigation and adaptation policies regarding climate change in the context of different scenarios, and each scenario is depicted by a storyline of a different future, as explained further below. In order to capture the climate change impacts in the SSPs, RCP 4.5 is selected and integrated in the scenarios of interest (**Table 1**). The main assumption of RCP 4.5 is that the carbon dioxide concentration will reach 650 CO_2 eq.; the radiative forcing is stabilised at approximately 4.5 W/m^2 and both will be stabilised after [2].

As presented by [3], all pathways are followed by a number of assumptions enhancing their storyline. In brief, the SSP1 depicts the sustainability scenario, where the technological change is rapid with the development goals being achieved while a path of sustainability that moves towards a less intensive use of resources is followed including lower carbon energy sources and high productivity of land. On the other side, SSP5 represents a fossil-fuelled economy, where in the absence of climate policies, energy demand is high and most of this demand is met with carbon-based fuels. Investments in alternative energy technologies are low, and there are few readily available options for mitigation. However, economic development is relatively rapid and itself is driven by high investments in human capital. Improved human capital also produces a more equitable distribution of resources, stronger institutions, and slower population growth, leading to a less vulnerable world better able to adapt to climate impacts.

The SSP2 or the business-as-usual pathway follows a consistency with the experience of the last century pattern of action. In particular, it illustrates a world, where social, economic and technological trends do not shift remarkably from historical patterns. Socio-economic progress and per capita income growth proceeds unevenly, with some countries developing rapidly while others fall short of expectations. Although sustainable development goals are a priority for global and national institutions, slow progress is made in achieving them. Environmental systems degrade, although there are some advancements, and overall, the intensity of resource and energy use declines. Global population growth is moderate increasing steadily across the twenty-first century. Income inequality persists or improves only

Factor	SSP1	SSP2	SSP5
Population growth	Low	Medium	Low
Urbanisation	High	Medium	High
Education level	High	Medium	High
Equity	High	Medium	High
Economic growth	High	Medium, uneven	High
Globalisation	Connected	Semi-open globalised	Strongly globalised
Policy focus	Sustainable development	Weak focus on sustainability	Free markets, human capital
Institutions	Effective	Modest effective	Effective
Technology development	Rapid	Medium, uneven	Rapid
Energy sources	Renewables	Fossil fuels	Fossil fuels
Energy intensity	Low	Uneven	High
Environmental impacts (policy focus)	Low	Continued degradation	Highly engineered
Challenge to mitigation (policy focus)	Low	Medium	High
Challenge to adaptation (policy focus)	Low	Medium	Low
Natural capital (policy focus)	Very high	Medium/low	Medium
Manufactured capital (industry)	High	Medium	High
Financial capital (industry/ GDP)	Medium/high	Medium	Very high
Social capital	High	Medium	Very high
Human capital	Medium/high	Medium	Very high

Table 1.
Summary of the main trends in important factors in the SSP.

slowly and challenges to diminishing vulnerability to societal and environmental changes remain.

In this chapter, the SSP2 is explicitly presented through a number of socio-economic indexes projected and analysed, while SSP1 and SSP5 will be discussed qualitatively at the end of each section in comparison with the baseline, i.e. the SSP2. To stay as close as possible to the storyline of the SSPs, the main trends and assumptions have been downscaled for each scenario in **Table 1**. For example, population growth in SSP2 is assumed to be moderated, while in the other two scenarios, it is assumed that the growth rate will be lower, indicating a gentler slope. More details regarding the downscaling of the SSPs are provided within the following sections.

3. Demographic projections within ZRB boundaries

The ZRB is shared by eight riparian countries, each with a different area within ZRB. The biggest part is occupied by Zambia followed by Angola, Zimbabwe and Mozambique (see **Figure 1**). In this section, an estimation of the population within ZRB is demonstrated as developed in [5], considering social factors such as

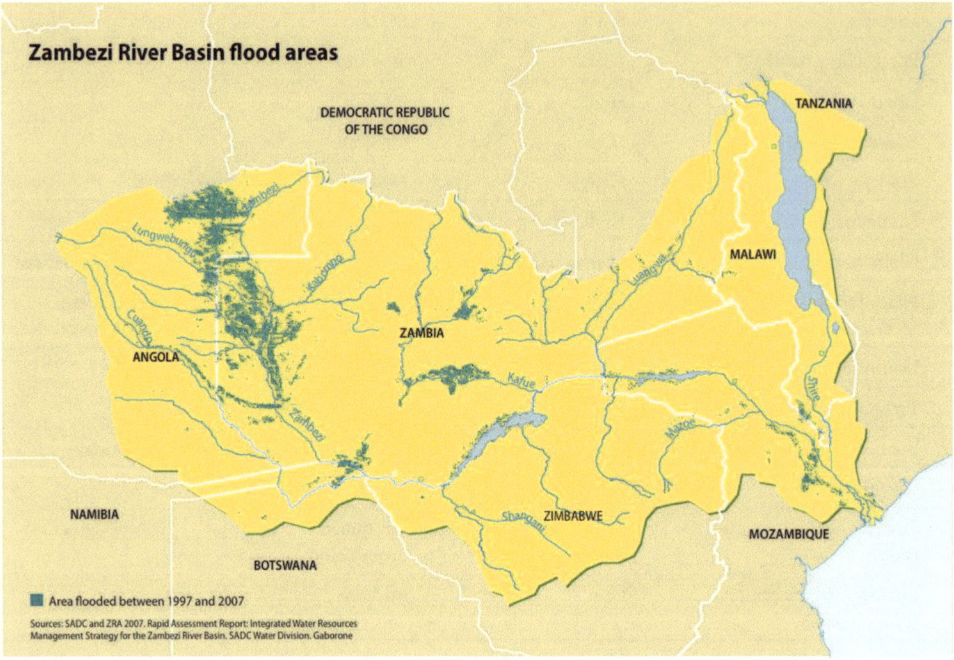

Figure 1.
Zambezi river basin (source: [4]).

mortality, fertility, international migration and urbanisation for the period from 2018 to 2060. The analysis below is based on the SSP2 scenario, which illustrates the middle of the road scenario, assuming that population fertility and the urbanisation level are both medium levels. SSP1 and SSP5 are examined as a comparison to the SSP2 at the end of the section.

3.1 Population growth per country

Population growth by country is estimated and presented in **Figure 2**. In order to calculate those trends, a simple model with one lag considering the values of the previous year and the annual population growth rates per country is run. A comprehensive and transparent selection of the growth rates was an important stage of this exercise, due to its impact on the future trends. After comparing a number of resources, population growth rates provided by [6] seem to have the most transparent and analytical approach. A crucial benefit of this report is not only the 100-year

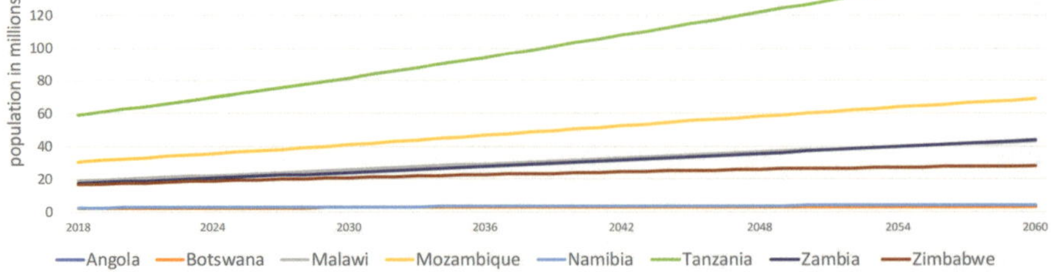

Figure 2.
Population growth by country.

forward looking but also the time slice of the predictions to 5-year periods, which enables projections to be comparatively more accurate. In order to be in alignment with SSP2 pathway, a population growth rate with constant mortality, normal international migration and median fertility assumptions is selected among the 10 indices provided in [6].

In Tanzania, population is proceeding apace in the next 40 years and it is expected to more than double, reaching almost 150 million people, which is of exceptional importance. However, such an enormous population increase would be accompanied by high concentration in major urban cities. Although only one urban city of Tanzania (as urban centres are considered cities with a population greater than 100,000 inhabitants), Katumba, located at the borders of Malawi, is identified within ZRB area, intra-urban agglomeration effects may be noticed increasing so the intensions over the water use of the river. Moreover, Malawi and Zambia, which together have as many inhabitants within ZRB as the rest of the countries jointly, seem to follow similar growth trends starting from 20 million to 18.6 million correspondingly and exceeding 43 million people each by 2060. Hence, the increased needs for water from half of the ZRB population are increasing, but not rapidly in the following 30 years enabling so, factors such as innovation and precautions to play a considerable role.

3.2 Population growth per major urban centre

Major urban centres are outlined by large populations, intensive economic activity and infrastructural development, which inevitably impose a significant strain on natural resources and especially water. Out of the 56 major urban centres with population greater than 100,000 identified for all riparian countries, 19 are geographically located within the boundaries of the ZRB. This chapter presents the population increase of these 19 major cities and the transition of smaller cities into major urban centres within ZRB boundaries during the period of interest.

The estimation of the demographic development for each riparian city is based on the data derived by [7] regarding their population levels in 2018 and by annual population and urbanisation growth rates provided by [6, 8]. **Figure 3** illustrates the population projections by major cities within ZRB, with Lusaka (Zambia) and Harare (Zimbabwe) reaching 3.2 million and 2.6 million people by 2060. The most

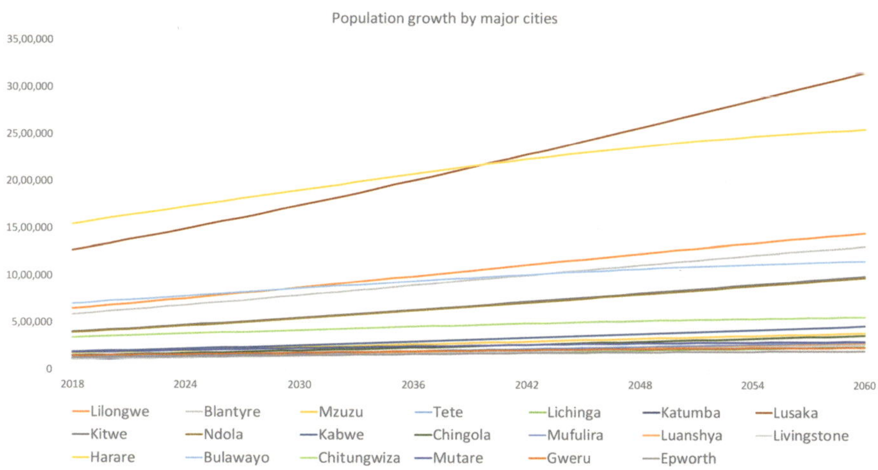

Figure 3.
Population growth by major urban centre.

populated riparian cities are located in Zambia, Zimbabwe and Malawi, with cities located in Mozambique and Tanzania following less vigorous growth. However, 12 non-major urban areas today will become significantly inhabited in the next 40 years attracting investments and necessary infrastructure in order to host the rising population. This transition will also be accompanied by additional pressure on water-energy-food supplies, the demand of which in urban areas tends to be significantly higher. Angola, Botswana and Namibia are not represented in the graph, since none of their major or potentially major cities is placed within ZRB area.

4. Domestic water-energy-food consumption projections within ZRB boundaries

4.1 Domestic future water requirements per country's share within ZRB area

Withdrawals for domestic uses include drinking water, municipal use or supply, and use for public services, commercial establishments and homes. In this section, the water consumption in the domestic sector for each country is estimated within the ZRB for the period 2016–2060. Data from [5, 7] and the previous section have been used to compute the projected water consumption by private households, where the annual water use per capita is multiplied with the population located in the ZRB for each riparian country.

As presented in **Figure 4**, the water use is expected to increase dramatically if we only consider the demographic growth of the riparian countries. Specifically, the total water use within ZRB is expected to reach 1.8 billion m^3 by 2060, while now it is approximately 0.8 billion m^3. What should be pointed out is that households in Zambia and Zimbabwe consume more water than in Malawi and Mozambique, although they are not dominating demographically within the basin, constituting 25 and 17% of the total population of the basin with the latter two occupying 29 and 24% correspondingly.

Today, most riparian countries withdraw less than 10% of their available freshwater resources, except of Zimbabwe, which withdraws almost 25% of its availability [9]. However, given the countries performance in improving water access as estimated by water, sanitation and hygiene (WASH) [10] only Zimbabwe and

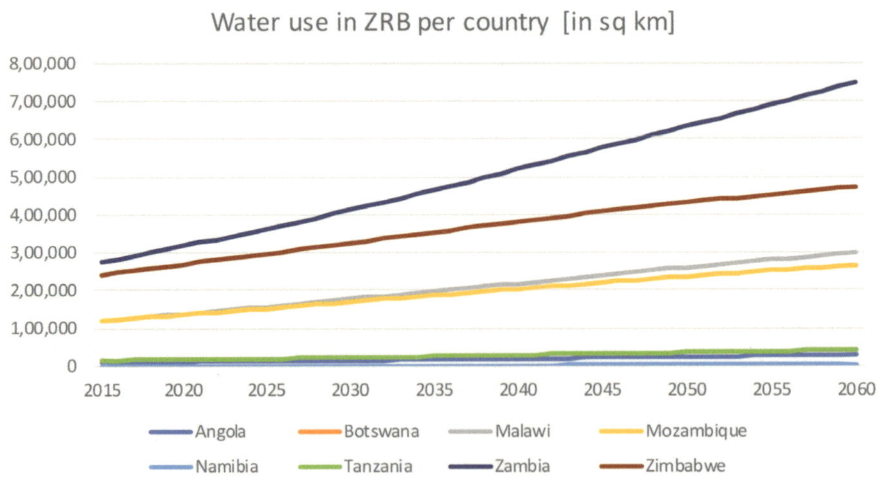

Figure 4.
Water use per country in m^3.

Tanzania are progressing, while Botswana, Malawi, Mozambique, Namibia and Zambia, which withdraw only from 1 to 11% of their freshwater availability are not on track of increasing their access to water, with Namibia having the worst performance. The water stress described above in combination with the climate change, which makes water availability less predictable in many places and it is associated with incidences of flooding, which threaten to destroy water points and sanitation facilities and contaminate water sources, could lead to even lower levels of access to water, increasing so the gap between water availability and water use, which is driven by the high increase of the population in the riparian countries. A lack in providing access to safe water, which is a fundamental human need, would drive protests putting pressure on the government from the society, which could lead in potential conflicts among neighbouring countries through competition for the limited supplies as a matter of national security.

4.2 Domestic future electricity requirements per country's share within ZRB area

As in the previous sector, the electricity consumption per capita in the domestic sector of each riparian country computed from [7] is used to estimate the annual electricity consumption per country's share within the ZRB for the domestic sector considering moderate urbanisation rates and the other SSP2 assumptions.

Figure 5 shows the projected electricity use for the period 2015–2060. By 2060, the total electricity consumption within ZRB is expected to reach 207 TWh, which is more than twice as much as it is today. As before, Zambians living within the ZRB are expected to consume in total more electricity than the inhabitants of Zimbabwe and Mozambique, not because of their demographic advantage, but because of their high electricity use per capita. However, Namibia and Botswana seem to use very low quantities of water for domestic purposes, due to their minor demographic share within ZRB and not due to their actual water needs.

4.3 Domestic future food requirements per country's share within ZRB area

In alignment with the previous two sectors, data for the daily calorie, protein and fat intake needs of an individual for each country from [11] are used to estimate

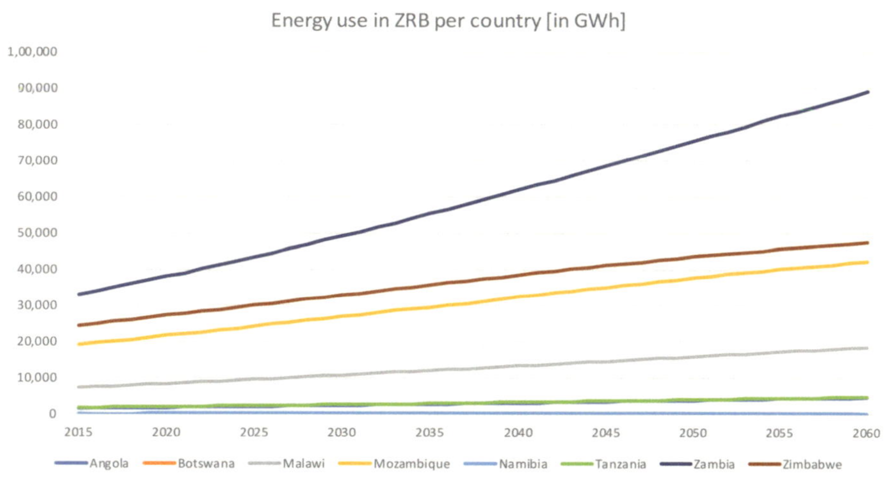

Figure 5.
Electricity use per country in GWh.

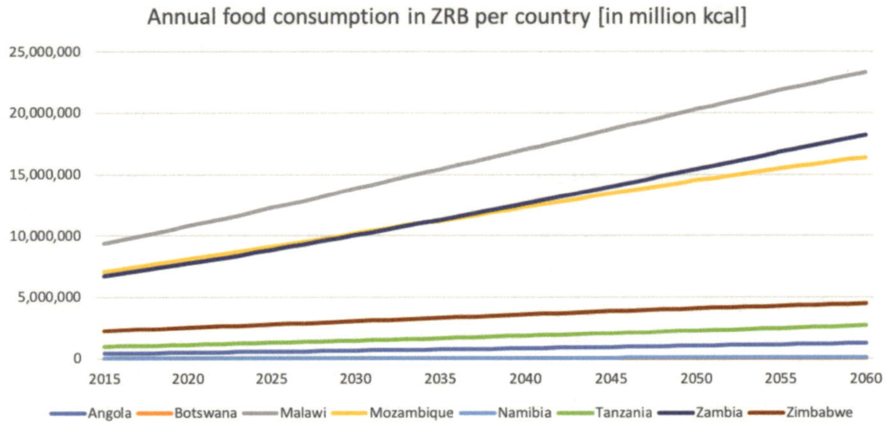

Figure 6.
Food consumption per country in million kcal.

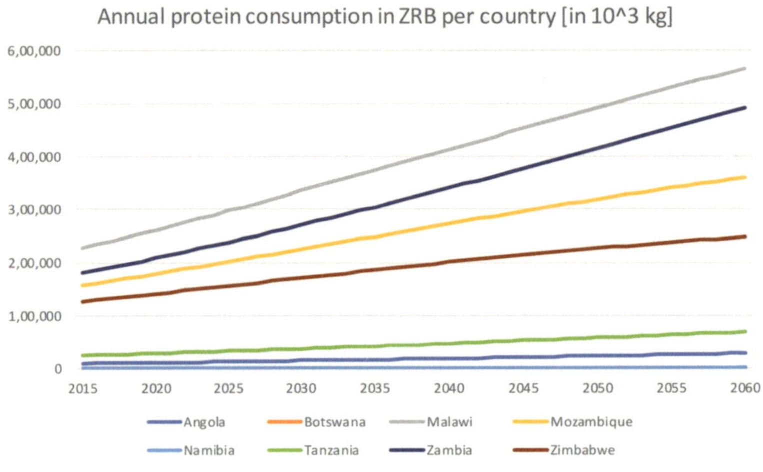

Figure 7.
Protein consumption per country in tonnes.

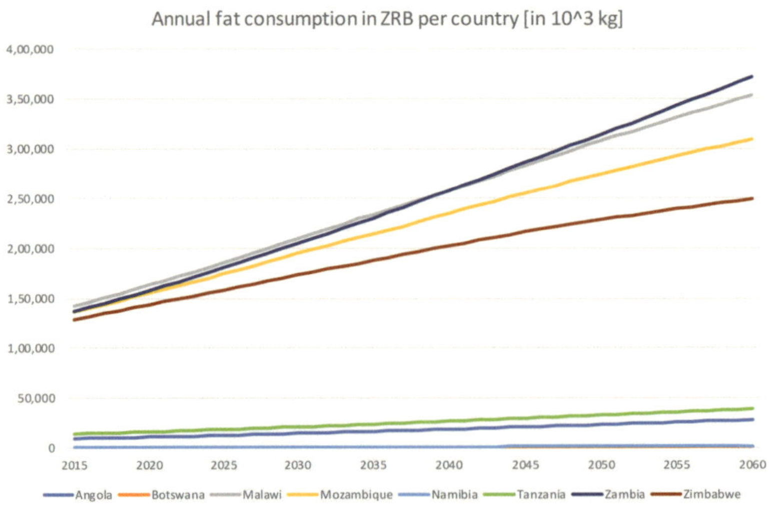

Figure 8.
Fat consumption per country in tonnes.

the long-term food demand. Based on these data, the annual food consumption per person is computed and multiplied with the population projections per country estimated in the previous chapter under SSP2 assumptions to obtain the estimates corresponding to the river basin scale. The outputs of these projections per national consumption of people living within the basin can be seen in **Figures 6–8**. The growth pattern does not change significantly among the graphs. In all graphs Malawi, Zambia and Mozambique have the greatest consumptions, with Malawi being the leader. In terms of total calorie intakes, the total expected consumption in ZRB in 2060 will reach 66.4 trillion calories, with Malawi consuming 35% of them. In terms of protein and fat intakes, the total consumption will reach 1.7 and 1.3 gigatonnes, respectively, with Malawi consuming 32 and 26% in each case.

5. Economic development

WEF future consumption is not only driven by demographic parameters, but by economic development as well. In order to understand the current economic situation and hence, the economic growth of the riparian countries under the SSP2 pathway, indices such Gross Domestic Value (GDP), GDP per capita, employment need to be investigated.

Short-term GDP projections (2018–2023) are based on GDP growth rates and data deriving by [9, 12], while long-term GDP projections (2023–2060) have been made using an AR(1) with one lag model (random walk) with constant slope using data from the post-war period from 1980 to 2017. However, the uncertainty associated with the long-term projections and the intense growth of the riparian countries in the recent future influences significantly the projections making them unreliable after year 2040. The reason why 2040 is selected as a turning point is that no specific plans are available for the period following and hence, a remarkably rapid growth could not be justified neither by development plans nor by past data. Hence, for the period 2040–2060 proxies from other similar countries (in terms of development) are used through splitting the period in decades and using different growth rates.

The growth in the period 2018–2040 will be significantly high, since in this period, the development is enhanced by the 2030 development goals of those countries and the international movements for better life standards in African countries. For example, universal, affordable and sustainable access to WASH is a key public health issue within international development and the main focus of Sustainable Development Goal 6 (SDG 6). According to the performance statistics for 2015, Tanzania and Zimbabwe are placed among the high-performing countries, while Namibia among the low-performing countries [10]. Hence, the GDP growth rates must be in alignment with these ratings until 2030, with high-performing countries growing faster (p.es. Tanzania's GDP is growing with 8.3% rate) than the low-performing countries (p.es. Namibia's GDP is growing with 4.7%).

As presented in **Figure 9**, Angola's GDP is almost as high as the GDP of all the other riparian countries combined, reaching $125 billion in 2017. However, its GDP growth (18%) over the 7-year period from 2017 to 2023 is not as high as the one in the other countries. According to [13], growth in Angola will accelerate, as a result of increased industrial activity and improving energy supplies, while the new administration of President João Lourenço is committed to restoring macroeconomic stability and implementing reforms. Since the last year's election, the administration has started to implement relevant policies including dismissing officials linked to the previous administration, launching investigations into possible misappropriation of funds at several public entities, and creating a specialised anti-corruption unit. Additionally, the impact of a dramatic drop in oil prices that

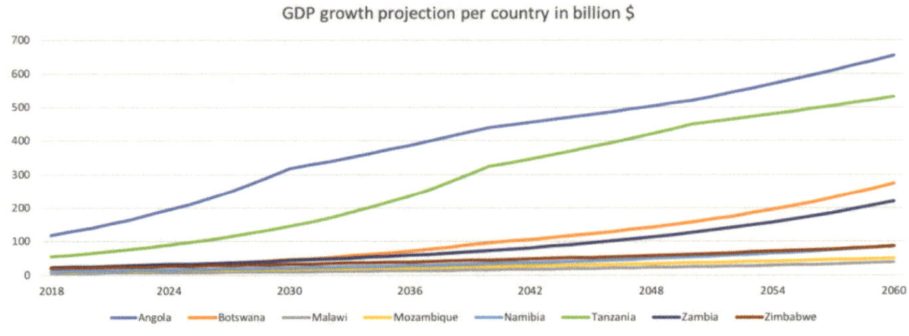

Figure 9.
GDP growth projections per country.

started in mid-2014 in the economy led the officials to address vulnerabilities more forcefully and diversify the economy away from oil, including a significant—17½% of GDP—improvement in the non-oil primary fiscal balance over 2015–2016 [14].

Economic growth in Botswana will be a result of advancements in all main sectors of the economy, but mainly by mineral prices. The outlook for the mining sector of Botswana is positive due to an anticipated increase in demand for Botswana's rough diamonds, with diamonds comprising 75% of the country's total exports. The non-mining sectors are also expected to pick up further, driven by structural reforms, including an amended immigration law that ensures rattling processing of work and residence permits and a move that provides utilities at reasonable prices to encourage domestic manufacturers. Construction is anticipated to continue being benefited by the on-going fiscal stimulus [15].

Prospects have been enhanced in Malawi after the reestablishment of its relations with foreign donors. Malawi's growth ensues from agricultural improvements, stable macroeconomic fundamentals, the recovery in global commodity prices and continued foreign direct investment inflows [15]. However, weather-related shocks are key risks to export commodities such as tea, tobacco and other products, as experienced in 2017, due to high dependence on rain-fed agriculture. The long dry spell in the first half of 2018 and fall 2018's armyworm infestation reduced the maize output, contributing substantially to GDP deceleration in 2018.

Additionally, Magufuli's presidency in Tanzania is expected to create the necessary circumstances for a boost in economic performance of the country, such as road building or fighting corruption. As reported by [14], economic growth in Tanzania has been relatively strong in the past decade resulting from wise macroeconomic policies and consecutive Fund programs, which contributed to low inflation and contained public sector debt.

In Zimbabwe, policy-related macroeconomic instability remains a key challenge for private sector development. In particular, the macroeconomic instability is related to lack of funding, land tenure and investment regulations, high-input costs and outdated machinery, inefficient government bureaucracy, and inadequate infrastructure (particularly energy). However, the country has one of the most youthful populations consisting of 36% of the total population, with the population ages 15–34 [15]. The agricultural sector and mining are expected to be the main drivers of growth, backed by increased public and private investment. Lastly, the government has adopted and is implementing prudent fiscal policy underpinned by adherence to fiscal rules reprioritizing capital expenditure through commitment to increase the budget on capital expenditures from 16% of total budget expenditures in 2018 to over 25% in 2019 and 2020.

The medium-term outlook of Namibia is mixed. Aggregate demand is expected to recover steadily, as private activity picks up and new infrastructure projects are implemented as part of the stimulus package. Growth will also be driven by increased capacity utilisation in a new uranium mine as well as by improved business confidence, since reforms are accelerated. However, growth could remain weak if growth in key trading partners, such as South Africa, continues to be slow or if international prices of Namibia's commodity exports fall. Uncertainty over land reform and the economic empowerment agenda could also constrain the growth outlook. The government's assurance that land will not be expropriated without compensation should help ease such concerns.

Investment in Mozambique is being delayed by the government's default in January 2017 and the increased debt, while growth in Mozambique will additionally be restrained due to political tensions. Recently, a massive popular protest against fuel price increases has taken place. On top of that, downside risks to Mozambique's economic growth include rising prices for key imports such as fuel and food and economic difficulties in South Africa, Mozambique's second largest export destination. Lastly, according to [15], Mozambique's public debt is in distress and failure to agree on restructuring debt and restoring investor confidence could deepen economic hardship and slow growth.

The persisting dependence of Zambia's growth on the price of copper, which fell by more than 18% in 2018, will be restrained by deficiencies in the electricity supply, 97% of which is generated by hydropower, and by lower demand from China associated with escalating trade tensions [13, 15]. To improve investor confidence in Zambia and hence, debt sustainability, which is another key challenge of Zambia's economy, the government announced measures aimed at improving debt sustainability and returning to a rating of moderate risk of debt distress. The measures include an indefinite postponement of new infrastructure projects and the cancellation of some contracted loans that are yet to disburse.

However, considering the historical data of all riparian countries—except of Botswana, which is one of Africa's most stable countries with continuous multiparty democracy—political instability is increased driving so the levels of uncertainty attached to the projections of these countries higher. The estimations of [12] show that by the end of 2023, the GDP in Tanzania, Malawi and Mozambique will be increased by 45, 35 and 35% correspondingly, probably due to expected improvements in the political system of those countries, which have been associated with mismanagement, pressure on the media and corruption. Malawi's elections will take place with three competing parties in May 21st, 2019, Mozambique's elections in October 2019, Tanzania's elections are scheduled in 2020 [16].

In terms of WEF nexus, GDP growth can be constrained or accelerated by water, energy and food risks. Increasing GDP could increase further the demand for water, energy and food, as more and more people could afford to consume higher quantities of these goods. Consequently, an increased burden could be placed on the management of the resources, which except of smoothing people's lives are also initial inputs for the economic growth. Hence, if they are not managed efficiently, they could even slow down the growth of the economy.

6. Water-energy consumption projections per economic sector within ZRB boundaries

6.1 GDP composition

Water and energy are significant inputs of all sectors of the economy. In this case, the economy is assumed to be driven by three main sectors: agriculture, industry and services. The current share of each sector to the GDP of each riparian

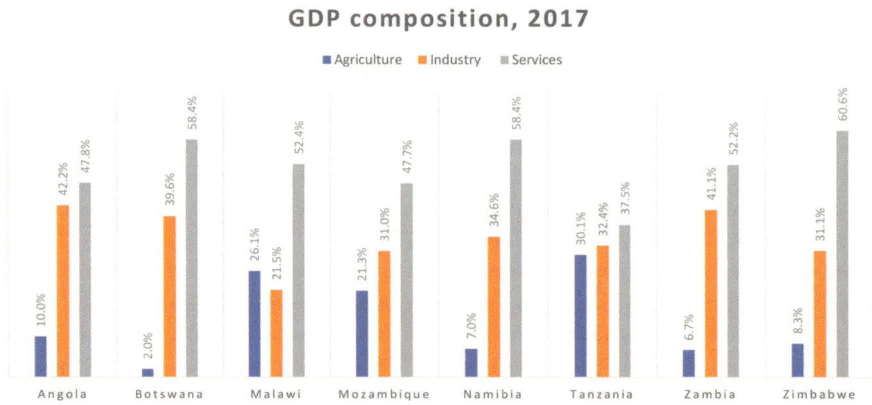

Figure 10.
GDP composition per country, 2017 (source: [9]).

country in terms of added value is illustrated in **Figure 10**, with *agriculture sector* including forestry and fishing, *industry sector* including construction and data deriving by [9]. Services is the driving sector of the economy of all riparian countries, as presented in **Figure 10**. In particular, it skyrockets in Zimbabwe reaching 61%, while it takes its lowest value in Tanzania with only 38% GDP share. In terms of agriculture, only Tanzania, Malawi and Mozambique have a considerable presence in the economy, while comparatively Angola (the second largest oil producers in Africa), Zambia (the second largest copper producer in Africa after Congo) and Botswana (one of the world's major diamond producers) are more industrial countries.

6.2 Future water requirements per economic sector

The water use associated with the industrial, agricultural and service sectors differs significantly not only across the sectors, but across countries as well. It is clear that the majority of freshwater withdrawals occur within industry sector, the annual consumption of which in 2017 varied from 13 billion cubic meters in Namibia to 611 billion cubic meters in Angola. Such a difference is not attributed to the difference in their industry sector's share of added value to their GDP, which is only 8%, but to their vast GDP difference, which implies a significant disparity in the size of the industry sector in each country. Indeed, according to the World Bank [9], the value of the industry sector in Angola is $52.3 billion, which is four times higher than the annual GDP of Namibia.

In order to compare the annual water consumption of the three sectors, we can consider the average water use in 2017 of the aggregated water consumptions of the eight riparian countries in each sector. As shown above, almost all freshwater withdrawals are consumed by the industry sector, which on average needs 134.5 billion cubic meters per year, while the agriculture needs only 1.1 billion cubic meters and the service sector less than 0.3 billion cubic meters. In order to come up with these numbers, data from [9] are used for annual freshwater withdrawals per sector to calculate the water use in billion cubic meters per 1% of added value in the GDP. Due to lack of data, this step was necessary in order to get an average water use per country, compute the current values and estimate the total water use per sector and per country.

Another interesting aspect of the water use per sector is its projection in the future. Considering the trends on GDP composition projection estimated in [5] and the average water use per sector and country, annual projections

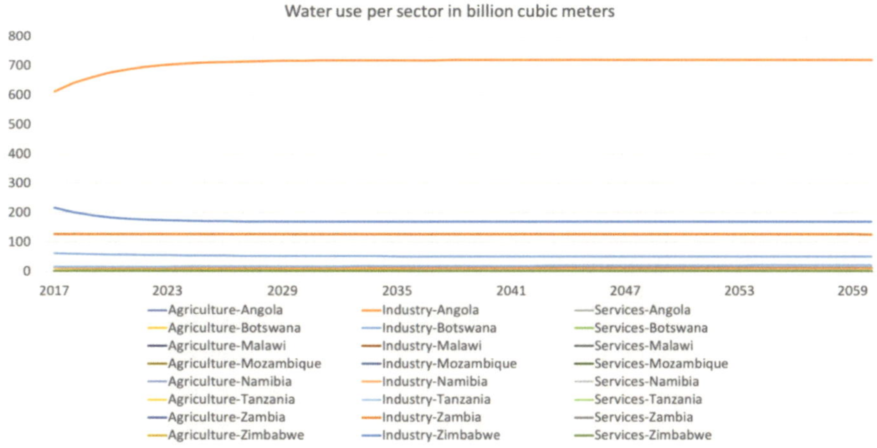

Figure 11.
Water use projections per sector per country.

have been computed and illustrated in **Figure 11**. As SSP2 scenario commands, without any dramatic changes in the distribution of the economy of the riparian countries, water use will keep on being extremely high for the industry sector of Angola, Zambia and Zimbabwe varying between 126 and 719 billion cubic meters in 2060.

As described in the previous section, access to freshwater is a crucial aspect of how future needs will be met. In terms of economic sectors, traditionally agriculture seems to require the majority of freshwater withdrawals at the most riparian countries with the range from 70 to 89% of the total withdrawals of each country. This means that in some countries, the economic activity of which is based on the agriculture, such as Tanzania, Malawi and Mozambique, will be highly sensitive on water withdrawal fluctuations as a result of increased population, low improvement rates of water access and climate change [9, 10]. A decrease in the economic activity deriving from agriculture would not only lower the GDP of the country but increase significantly the unemployment rates and the potential conflicts between the riparian countries in regards with the dominance over the freshwater supplies. Historically, water supply systems have been the objectives of military action and instruments of war, as water demand increases and water supply becomes more problematic and uncertain as a result of global climate change.

6.3 Future energy requirements per economic sector

In order to replace mainstream sources of energy with more efficient and better targeted social safety nets for the most vulnerable energy sources, some countries make significant use of subsidies. In particular, as presented in [15]. Zimbabwe, Zambia and Mozambique received the highest subsidies among the other African countries. In Zambia, mining output is expected to increase by 4–5% in 2019, benefiting from improvements in electricity generation associated with the replenishment of the Kariba Dam due to good weather conditions [15].

Aiming to boost domestic supply of local products, some of the riparian countries chose more conservative policies, such as banning imports or implementing tariffs. For instance, Botswana, Zambia, and Zimbabwe ban imports of poultry, maize meal and cooking oil, while Zimbabwe's competition and tariff by-laws require supermarkets to buy domestically at least 20% of the goods they are selling.

As far as these policies are being performed, domestic agriculture, fishing and animal husbandry will be boosted by facing a comparatively more protected demand and fair prices.

Mozambique could become one of the largest exporters of natural gas in the world by 2020 (the country hosts the third largest reserve in Africa) thanks to the discovery of new reserves. Lastly, the planned construction of natural gas plants as well as a new dam should allow the country to increase its electricity exports to neighbouring countries. Export infrastructure (railroads, deep water ports, liquefied natural gas plants) is also under construction. The country is expected to export natural gas and coal to Asia by 2020.

7. Summary of SSPs

In this chapter, a future scenario for eight riparian countries has been developed and presented explicitly, while two more scenarios have been analysed in comparison with the baseline scenario, SSP2.

7.1 Summary of middle of the road scenario (SSP2)

7.1.1 Society

This path follows a pattern of action that is consistent with the experience of the last century. Under this scenario, the ZRB can expect to see the total population living within the basin after considering urbanisation trends to reach 99 million people by 2060 with 3 million of them being due to urbanisation assumptions. Education levels are moderate limiting so, the social and human capital of the riparian countries, but explaining the significant increase in the population.

7.1.2 WEF nexus

As presented in the previous sections above, water, energy and food consumptions within ZRB are expected to increase significantly by 2060, due to high population growth. The total water use within ZRB is expected to increase up to 1.8 billion m^3 from 0.8 billion m^3, which is the current value, while the climate change in combination with the water stress could increase the gap between water demand and supply. The total energy consumption within ZRB is expected to reach 207 TWh by 2060, which is more than twice as much as it is today. In terms of total calorie intakes, the total expected consumption in ZRB in 2060 will reach 66.4 trillion calories, with Malawi consuming 35% of them. In terms of protein and fat intakes, the total consumption will reach 1.7 and 1.3 Gigatonnes, respectively, with Malawi consuming 32 and 26% in each case.

7.1.3 Economy

In SSP2, although all countries are developing, some of them are making greater progress than the others. Given the historical patterns, the forecasting shows that Angola, Tanzania and Botswana, which are relatively richer in absolute values than Malawi and Namibia, are expected to increase with a higher pace (around 8%) than the other countries, which can accelerate with rate between 3.3 and 5.3%. Hence, existing inequalities are increasing more and more creating a greater gap between developing and developed world. Economic growth is followed by increased employment as well, with agriculture sector playing a significant role in that trend.

7.1.4 Climate change

Limited pro-active initiatives are considered from both Government and institutions in SSP2. The world is semi-open globalised, while the policies do not prioritise sustainability and the institutions are modestly effective. On top of that, extensive use of fossil fuels leads to continued degradation of the environmental assets, while the challenge to mitigate or adapt to these effects is moderate.

7.2 Alternative SSPs: SSP1 and SSP5

While the previous sections depict in detail the SSP2 scenario, where global development follows a middle of the road path, this section considers two alternative futures under SSP1 and SSP5. SSP1 is perceived as the sustainable pathway focusing on the role of the environmental services in the economy, while SSP5 is the economically driven scenario, which, although recognises the economic impacts of the environmental degradation on the economy, does not take pro-active actions, but it focuses on technology improvements able to mitigate the skyrocketed emissions of the human activity.

7.2.1 Sustainability conscious scenario (SSP1)

7.2.1.1 Society

SSP1 envisions a development path with increased investment in education and health. Hence, greater access to education is leading to a relatively rapid demographic transition, due to birth controls and lower child mortality rates, which tones down the moderate population growth noted in SSP2, and also increases the human and social capital of the economy [17]. By contrast, urbanisation is assumed to be rapid in SSP1, which drives high income growth. Under this scenario, urbanisation is desired given the high efficiency that compact urban areas may achieve.

7.2.1.2 WEF nexus

WEF projections would also diversify in the SSP1 and SSP5 as a result of different population inputs. In particular, since the population will decrease and that the urbanisation levels will remain as high as in SSP2, the final population within the basin will be significantly lower and hence the needs for water, energy and food will not increase dramatically.

7.2.1.3 Economy

The main feature of this narrative is the achievement of development goals while following a path of sustainability that moves towards a less intensive use of resources. As presented in **Table 1**, the economic development in SSP1 is expected to be high, with GDP growing more rapidly than the one illustrated in **Figure 9**. The drive of economic growth in this scenario is the fact that the human well-being is redefined in SSP1 considering the environmental services, which are included in the economic development initiatives and in the overall shift of the economy to environmentally friendly actions with the help of rapid technology improvements. Employment in SSP1 will also be rapid following the great economic development of the countries, overpassing the levels of SSP2.

7.2.1.4 Climate change

By contrast, in SSP1, sustainable development is the central focus of all policies across the world, which is connected in decision-making with strong and effective institutions. Renewable sources of energy lead to an optimal treatment of the natural capital, while the need for mitigation or adaptation remains low.

7.2.2 Fossil fuel-driven scenario (SSP5)

7.2.2.1 Society

Similarly to SSP1, SSP5 envisions a development path with increased investment in education and health. Hence, greater access to education is leading to a relatively rapid demographic transition, due to birth controls and lower child mortality rates, which tones down the moderate population growth noted in SSP2, and also increases the human and social capital of the economy [17]. By contrast, urbanisation is assumed to be extremely rapid in SSP5, driving high-income growth. Cities attract migration due to other reasons from SSP1, such as rapid technological change allowing for large-scale engineering projects to develop desirable housing.

7.2.2.2 WEF nexus

WEF projections in this scenario would also diversify than SSP2 as a result of different population inputs. Likewise SSP1 case, population per country will decrease, revealing so the water, energy and food needs per person will also decrease. However, in this case, the urbanisation levels are more rapid than the other two paths, which means that the final population within the basin can be as much as in SSP2 declaring so the similar needs for water, energy and food.

7.2.2.3 Economy

The main characteristic of this narrative is the rapid development of the economy and the intensive use of fossil fuels. As presented in **Table 1**, the economic development in SSP1 is expected to be high, with GDP growing more rapidly than the one illustrated in **Figure 9**. However, the economic strategy of this scenario differs considerably than the SSP1 and SSP2, letting so GDP growth rates take their highest possible values. Innovation and investments are the most preferable options in SSP5, where technological progress and competitive markets drive growth. Employment in this scenario will also be rapid following the great economic development of the countries.

7.2.2.4 Climate change

In SSP5, free markets and emphasis on human capital drive the economy under a strongly globalised status quo administrated by effective institutions. High economic growth driven by energy based on fossil-fuels leads to increases in GHG emissions and so, great mitigation challenges. However, although the dominance of fossil fuels impacts significantly the environment, it does not degrade it more than SSP1, due to high mitigation policies, which control environmental processes through highly engineered systems, nevertheless with no focus on adaptation.

8. Conclusions

This section presented extensively projections regarding different aspects of the SSP2 scenario and then it compared them to SSP1 and SSP5 scenarios for two case studies. The SSP2 scenario illustrates the case, where the global development follows a middle of the road path, with most variables taking moderate values; the SSP1 describes a sustainable pathway focusing on the role of the environmental services in the economy, while SSP5 focuses on the economic progress only, where negative externalities on the environment are treated as a cost and hence mitigated. Demographic and economic indicators have been populated and forecasted, among which are lying population projections per country/major and potentially major city, WEF projections per country within ZRB area, GDP, GDP composition and projections until 2060.

In demographic terms, the total population living within ZRB is clearly affected by a moderate urbanisation trend as assumed in SSP2, while education levels are moderate limiting so the social and human capital of the riparian countries. In SSP1 and SSP5, access to education is greater leading so to birth control, which tones down the moderate population growth noted in SSP2, and also increases the human and social capital of these economies. By contrast, urbanisation is assumed to be rapid in both SSP1 and SSP5, which drives high-income growth. Note, however, that in SSP1, urbanisation is desired given the high efficiency that compact urban areas may achieve, while in SSP5, cities attract migration due to other reasons, such as rapid technological change allowing for large-scale engineering projects to develop desirable housing.

In economic terms, although all countries are developing, some of them are making greater progress than the others, driving existing inequalities to increase more and more and leave a greater gap between developing and developed world. However, although the economic development in both SSP1 and SSP5 is expected to be high, it will be more balanced than in SSP1 scenario decreasing so the existing inequalities. Note, though that the high-economic growth illustrated in the former scenarios is originated from two diametrically opposed strategies. Human well-being is redefined in SSP1 considering the environmental services, which lead development initiatives and the overall shift of the economy towards environmentally friendly actions with the help of rapid technology improvements. On the other side, innovation and investments are the most desirable options in SSP5, where growth is driven by technological progress and competitive markets. However, high fossil-fuel reliance in alignment with the high economic growth leads to higher GHG emissions and hence, higher mitigation challenge.

Lastly, in terms of climate change, limited pro-active initiatives are considered from both Government and institutions in SSP2. The semi-open globalised political environment in addition with the modestly effective institutions fails to prioritise policies regarding sustainability. On top of that, extensive use of fossil fuels leads to continued degradation of the environmental assets, while mitigation and adaptation challenges are moderate. In contrast, in SSP1 sustainable development is the central focus of all policies across the world, which is connected in decision-making with strong and effective institutions. Renewable sources of energy lead to an optimal treatment of the natural capital, while the need for mitigation or adaptation remains low. In SSP5, free markets and emphasis on human capital drive the economy under a strongly globalised status quo administrated by effective institutions. The dominance of fossil fuels impacts significantly the environment, but it does not degrade it more than SSP1, due to high mitigation policies, which control environmental processes through highly engineered systems, nevertheless with no focus on adaptation.

The impact of climate change on access to freshwater will be highly visible under the SSP2 scenario, where the population growth is higher than the other two scenarios and no dramatic improvements in infrastructure are taken. However, the SSP1 scenario seems to handle in the best possible way the climate change uncertainty by having low population growth and increased access to water due to investments, while the SSP1 climate change impacts would be closer to the SSP2, as although population increase with lower to SSP2 rates, the investments in fossil fuels will increase CO_2 emissions, making the climate change impacts more extreme. In addition to the above, improving standards of living would increase further the water requirements of the citizens widening the gap between demand and supply in all three scenarios. Water scarce will increase competition over water supply driving so the political and societal instability within and between the countries.

Energy and food sectors will also be affected by the climate change as they are both based on water access. Hence, under SSP2 and SSP5, energy and food sectors will be significantly disturbed enhancing potential conflicts and wars between the countries as a result of social pressure. SSP1 seems to be the only case, where the adverse effects of climate change are mitigated as a result of the increased investments in water access and lower use of carbon-intensive technologies, as the oil price is high, and renewable energy gets competitive against fossil fuels.

This study has potential limitations. The projections taken place in the model are based on international organisations and studies. Moreover, the lack of data constituted the necessary use of proxies of other similar cases, simplifying so, the individuality of each country. Last but not least, the long-term time horizon is accompanied with great uncertainty. The projections are therefore subject to biases and confounding that may have influenced the results of this section. The breakdown in shorter terms of the indicators analysed in this study could give a more precise understanding of the future status quo in the two CS.

Acknowledgements

This work is supported by the Decision Analytic Framework to explore the water-energy-food nexus in complex transboundary water resource systems of fast developing countries (DAFNE) project, which has received funding from the European Union's Horizon 2020 research and innovation programme under grant agreement no. 690268. Comments from two anonymous reviewers greatly improved the manuscript.

Author details

Phoebe Koundouri[1,2,3,4*] and Lydia Papadaki[1,2,5]

1 Athens University of Economics and Business, Greece

2 EIT Climate-KIC Hub, Greece

3 United Nations Sustainable Development Network, Greece

4 European Association of Environmental and Natural Resource Economists, Italy

5 UN SDSN, Greece

*Address all correspondence to: pkoundouri@aueb.gr

References

[1] Kriegler E, O'Neill BC, Hallegatte S, Kram T, Lempert R, Moss R, et al. The need for and use of socio-economic scenarios for climate change analysis: A new approach based on shared socio- economic pathways. Global Environmental Change. 2012;**22**:807-822

[2] Wayne GP. The Beginner's Guide to Representative Concentration Pathways. 2013. Available from: http://www.gci.org.uk/RCPs/RCP_Guide.pdf

[3] O'Neill B, Kriegler E, Riahi K, Ebi K, Hallegatte S, Carter T, et al. A new scenario framework for climate change research: The concept of shared socioeconomic pathways. Climatic Change. 2013;**122**(3):387-400. DOI: 10.1007/s10584-013-0905-2

[4] United Nations. GRID Arendal. 2019. Available from: http://www.grida.no/resources/5169

[5] DAFNE. Deliverable 2.2. 2019b. Available from: https://dafne.ethz.ch/results/deliverables/

[6] United Nations. Department of Economic and Social Affairs, Population Division. World Population Prospects: The 2017 Revision, DVD Edition, 2017

[7] DAFNE. Deliverable 2.1, 2019a. Available from: https://dafne.ethz.ch/results/deliverables/

[8] United Nations. World urbanization prospects: The 2018 revision. In: Average Annual Rate of Change of the Urban Population by Region, Subregion and Country, 1950-2050 (percent). Department of Economic and Social Affairs, Population Division; 2018b Available from: https://population.un.org/wup/Download/

[9] World Bank, Data Bank. World Bank Open Data. Free and open access to global development data. 2018. Available from: https://data.worldbank.org

[10] WASH funders. WASH Performance Index Reveals Unexpected Leaders in Water and Sanitation Progress. 2019. Available from: http://washfunders.org/wash-performance-index-reveals-unexpected-leaders-in-water-and-sanitation-progress/

[11] Food and Agricultural Organisation (FAO). Food Supply kcal/capita/day, 2018. Available from: http://www.fao.org/faostat/en/#search/Food%20supply%20kcal%2Fcapita%2Fday

[12] IMF. Real GDP growth. Annual Percent Change, 2018b. Available from: https://www.imf.org/external/datamapper/NGDP_RPCH@WEO/OEMDC/ADVEC/WEOWORLD

[13] United Nations. World Economic Situation and Prospects Report. 2018a. Available from: https://www.un.org/development/desa/dpad/wp-content/uploads/sites/45/publication/WESP2018_Full_Web-1.pdf

[14] IMF. IMF Country Information, 2018a. Available from: https://www.imf.org/en/Countries

[15] African Development Bank (AfDB). African Economic Outlook 2019. 2019. ISBN 978-9938-882-87-2

[16] EISA. 2019 African Election Calendar, 2019. Available from: https://www.eisa.org.za/calendar2019.php

[17] Jones B, O'Neill BC. Spatially explicit global population scenarios consistent with the shared socioeconomic pathways. Environmental Research Letters. 2016;**11**(8):084003. DOI: 10.1088/1748-9326/11/8/084003

Chapter 4

Consequences of Herbicide Use in Rural Environments and Their Effect on Agricultural Workers

Ana Paola Balderrama-Carmona, Norma Patricia Silva-Beltrán, Luis Alberto Zamora Alvarez, Norma Patricia Adan Bante and Edgar Felipe Moran Palacio

Abstract

The herbicides are used frequently to fight the proliferation of weeds. The use of herbicides correlates with an improvement in agricultural yield, but the harm to the health of human populations is well established and has been demonstrated in numerous scientific studies. In many developing countries, farmers build their own homes, and this, along with the application of herbicides in their fields, increases their exposure, through both contact with skin and respiration. It is scientifically proven that herbicides cause infertility, kidney problems, endocrine disruption, apoptosis, cytotoxicity, and neurotoxic effects. Such diseases impact the quality of those affected, and naturally the contaminated environment negatively affects human health. This chapter focuses on revising the most relevant studies regarding the health effects on agricultural workers living in rural environments due to herbicide contamination and how to sustain the herbicide use.

Keywords: occupational health, herbicide pollution, quality of life, economic vulnerability, agriculture sustainability

1. Introduction

Agriculture has enormous global environmental repercussion and still is an important sector responsible for the greater part of the rural communities' income in developing countries [1]. Agricultural land occupies a third of the ice-free global land area, and it is expected that this percentage will rise due to increased demand for agricultural products to support the continued growth in the human population [2].

Agricultural practices can be harmful to human and surrounding ecosystems. The environmental/occupational exposure to agrochemicals (pesticide or fertilizers) has become a concern for human health [3]. Sixty percent of agrochemicals are used in the soil, and the others drain into the ground polluting the water supply; these chemicals are toxic for living organisms as they are absorbed by plants and successively accumulate in human tissue through biomagnifications of the food chain, causing human health and environment concerns [4]. Chemical pollutants are a serious and growing global problem. Pollution has become one of the greatest threats to humankind and is caused by their prevalence in water, on land, and in air.

At least 7 million people die as a result of air pollution, 842,000 from water pollution, and 420,000 from consuming contaminated food. In 2015, 9 million people died (16% of deaths worldwide) due to poor waste management, generating more deaths than AIDS, malaria, and tuberculosis together [5]. According to the World Health Organization (WHO), more than 1000 pesticides [6], among them the herbicides, fungicides, bactericides, and insecticides, are used agriculturally today; however, as many as 140,000 pesticides have been synthesized since 1950.

One global concern is that genetically modified seeds permit farmers to spray herbicides even during the growing season. This leaves their crops unharmed—primarily soybeans and corn—but also leaves them with carcinogenic levels of the systemic herbicide glyphosate [7], according to the International Agency for Research on Cancer (IARC) [8]. Actually, 90% of the soybean and corn seeds are herbicide resistant [7]. A huge list of commercial food products containing soy, corn, and honey maintains traces of herbicides; glyphosate has also been reported in oat products [9].

In addition to the trace exposure of herbicides in various foods, the greatest levels are in the agricultural fields. The herbicides can be classified according to their chemical structure as organophosphates, organochlorines, carbamates, and pyrethroids, comprising a large portion of herbicides in the overall market. In developing countries, the most common herbicides based on their popularity are glyphosate, paraquat, atrazine, and 2,4-D. The use of these chemicals is well adapted for rural workers because they are of low cost, replace manual weeding, and improve yields [10]. However, accidental exposure to herbicides can be highly dangerous to human beings and other living organisms, and training programs by the sellers of herbicides that inform workers of the risk of exposure due to direct contact with the chemicals do not exist [11]. FAO reported that 800 million individuals in the world are undernourished, of which 780 million live in developing regions. Therefore, the possible health effects from the use of herbicides, in these regions, are considered by locals as less significant compared to the importance of eradicating famine [1, 12]. Because of this, it is important to balance the use of herbicides and their possible effect on the environment and health and reach sustainability. This review aims to present the key problems that can occur due to the mismanagement of herbicides in developing countries and how these chemicals can affect the health of farmworkers.

2. Methodology

A literature search was conducted to describe the health effects on agricultural workers in rural environments due to herbicide exposure and contamination. The following data sources were used: Medline, EMBASE, Science Direct, PubMed, and Redalyc, with published studies not older than 10 years. The key terms of the search were about farmer's health and herbicide contamination, although the search was not restricted. After deleting duplicate records, all remaining retrieved references to the bibliographic search were selected using only the title and summary. Research with irrelevant topics was eliminated to focus on the articles of interest in our study. The results were organized according to the type of health disorder due to occupational exposure. Studies focused on how to support the use of herbicides were also considered. Two hundred and one articles were selected for review of their abstracts, and 101 were classified for full analysis. After the revision of these full texts, only 61 studies were finally cited in this paper.

This review analyzes the impact of the excessive use of herbicides on specific health disorders in exposed agricultural workers and the environment damage.

Many studies expose the health effects caused by herbicides; however, those in developing countries are rare. It is necessary to emphasize agriculture-related poor practices, the almost inexistent farmer training, and the health risk that this entails.

3. Environmental impact of bad practices on agriculture

The unpromising future of agriculture in developing countries faces many challenges as a result of social pressure, increased migration, labor shortages, climate change, and food insecurity and is now an accelerating phenomenon that has resulted in the use of inadequate herbicides and depletion of natural resources, in particular the soil [12].

These events have led to the erosion of natural resources due to overexploitation of soils, to meet the growing demand for food [13], resulting in the excessive use of herbicides. It is well known that a significant portion of the chemicals applied has proven to be excessive, expensive, and sometimes unnecessary. In several countries such as in Europe and Japan, the use has been reduced; however, in the rest of the world, it has even increased [1].

Globally, in environmental government instances of some countries, are established permissible limits of herbicides in water and soil, however, in developing countries herbicides are not monitored, or simply this standards do not exist; nevertheless, several studies have shown that herbicides and their derivative compounds contaminate natural resources such as water and soil, for example, aminomethylphosphonic acid (AMPA), a secondary compound of glyphosate, can persist for several years in the soil [14]. The relationship between herbicide environmental pollution and the risk of harm to health is caused by failure to apply the adequate quantity, frequency of the products and the resistance of pests to herbicides, which causes them to tend to be accumulated in soil and water, depending on their physicochemical nature and their dynamics of interaction with the environment [15].

Table 1 shows residual soil and water values from the most commonly used herbicides worldwide. The concentrations found exceed the maximum permissible levels by international laws [22]. The reported values are evidence of progressive accumulation, which represents a risk factor for human health.

Reference	Compound	Concentration	Country/year
[15]	2,4-D (dichlorophenoxyacetic acid)*	609 μg/kg	Brazil, 2013
[16]	Terbuthylazine*	37.6 μg/kg	Arable, 2015
[17]	Phenolic herbicide*	0.4 mg/kg	Bosnia, 2016
[18]	AMPA*	342.75 mg/kg	Mexico, 2018
[19]	Glyphosate+	27.8 μg/L	USA, 2013
[20]	Atrazine+	15.66 μg/L	USA, 2008
[21]	Glyphosate+	1.42 μg/L	Mexico, 2015
[18]	Glyphosate+ AMPA+	≤5 μg/L 36.8 μg/L	Mexico, 2018

The compounds with an asterisk (*) are found in soil samples, and those with a plus sign (+) are herbicides reported in water.

Table 1.
Occurrence of herbicides in soil and water samples.

4. Health effects on agricultural workers

Occupational health hazards usually refer to the materials and processes that have the potential to cause injury, sickness, and impaired health and affect the well-being and efficiency among workers. Occupational diseases may occur long after being exposed to occupational hazards, such as air contaminants and chemical, biological, physical, and ergonomic hazards, including psychosocial factors as well [5]. In agricultural trade, workers are exposed to numerous agricultural environment aerosols, including herbicides.

People who have been exposed to herbicides occupationally, or by eating foods or liquids containing herbicide residue, or for that matter inhaled herbicide-contaminated air, have experience a broad range of chronic health effects, including impaired neurobehavioral function (e.g., cognitive and behavioral disorders), Alzheimer's and Parkinson's diseases, hormone disruption, asthma, allergies, hypersensitivity, obesity, diabetes, hepatic lesions, kidney failure, multiple sclerosis, and cancer [3, 23–25].

4.1 Neurobehavioral problems

Many studies related to the occupational herbicide exposure of agricultural workers exist. Neurobehavioral symptoms among participants appear to be associated with cumulative exposure [26]. Pesticide poisoning and suicides are very high in developing countries and rural environments. Suicides influenced by pesticides have been largely reported among agricultural workers; evidence exists that indicates that pesticides induce such behavior [25, 27]. Some organophosphates, for example, paraquat and glyphosate, inhibit the cholinesterase activity in the nervous system, whereby this irreversible inhibition can produce cerebral damage such that cholinergic neurons are injured and can be responsible for neuropsychiatric and neurobehavioral disorders, including memory, cognitive, mental, emotional, motor, and sensory deficits [28].

It has long been established that Alzheimer's development is exacerbated from occupational exposure to organophosphates. Chin-Chan [29] determined that the risk of Alzheimer's is higher in those who have had occupational contact. The herbicides induce oxidative stress which in turn produces the activation of calpains and then caspases, a known link to Parkinson's disease [30].

4.2 Hormone disruption

The inhibition of acetylcholinesterase in the hypothalamus after organophosphate exposure alters the secretion rate of gonadotropin-releasing hormone by affecting the secretion of pituitary hormones that stimulate the gonads (gonadotrophic hormones), including folio-stimulating and luteinizing hormones. The relationship between exposure to pesticides and anomalies in the functional structure of the seminal cells was checked [31].

A relationship between hypothyroidism and the use of organochlorine insecticides, fungicides, and herbicides has been found [32]. The organophosphates, by themselves, are capable of interfering with endocrine function by inhibiting the binding of thyroid hormones to their corresponding receptors.

4.3 Respiratory and immune diseases

Occupational exposure to pesticides can represent a serious risk to the respiratory system. Spirometry was performed in workers occupationally exposed to pesticides in various developing countries and revealed a significant decrease in the lung function parameters [33]. Another study evaluated the association between allergic and non-allergic wheeze and pesticides and found significant differences than implicate organophosphates and pyrethroids that are commonly used in agricultural and residential settings with adverse respiratory effects [34].

The organophosphates can affect the immune response, including the production of antibodies and of interleukin 2, T-cell proliferation, decrease of CD5 cells, increase of CD26 and autoantibodies, alteration of Th1/Th2 cytokines, inhibition of NK cells and the lymphocyte-activated killer cells, and the cytotoxic activity of the T lymphocytes. The oxidative stress can be produced by a wide range of factors among which the pesticides are found [35]. In this sense, Simoniello [36] showed that agricultural workers of the Pampas region in Argentina exposed to pesticide mixtures presented modifications in the oxidative equilibrium and enzymatic alterations.

4.4 Metabolic complications

It has been shown that there is an association between exposure to pesticides and a high incidence of metabolic syndrome, insulin resistance, and diabetes. The pesticides affect the cellular metabolism of carbohydrates and lipids and can lead to insulin resistance and alterations in glucose homeostasis [37]. Organochloride compounds are persistent and remain in the body for a long period. The presence of multiple chlorine atoms in its structure increases its lipophilicity and results in accumulation in adipose tissue. Several studies have explored the possible relationship between the concentration of organochlorides and obesity [38].

Organochlorides are associated with peripheral arterial disease, particularly in people suffering from obesity, the idea being that dioxins are supported after binding to AhR and induce inflammation, hypertension, and arteriosclerosis [39].

5. Implications of herbicides on health problems in people who live in agricultural rural areas

The use of herbicides is uncontrolled in many developing countries. Herbicides can cause toxic effects on agricultural workers' health, both by their direct and indirect action (inhalation, dermal or oral exposure) [10]. Long-term and acute occupational exposure to herbicide among agricultural workers produces a charge or a cost to the countries [40]; the study of Buendía [41] reports that the average cost per patient intoxicated by paraquat exceeds that of various chronic diseases prevalent in Colombia. The social and economic impact on health could contribute significantly to the global public health problem. The increased morbidity includes lower quality of life and functional status.

The Organisation for Economic Co-operation and Development (OECD) offers "the Index for a Better Life" which measures people's quality of life and compares it among countries, based on the personalized management of the priorities of each individual [42]. In developing countries increase the poverty of the population, due to the low remuneration, for example, in the research of Cely-Andrade [43] reports that in mining zones exist the worst quality of life-related to health than agricultural areas, however the mining works are better paid, although economic growth does not accurately represent human well-being, the economic dimension is a key dimension of rural prosperity and farmers consider that economic resources increase the chances of improving their quality of life.

Reference	Method	Participants and precedence	Reported concentrations in urine
[38]	ELISA	Agricultural workers in Costa Rica	6.3 μg/24 h of paraquat
[44]	HPLC–MS/MS	Students in Thailand	2,4-D
[45]	ELISA	Children in Nicaragua	0.9 μg/g Cr 2,4-D
[46]	LC–MS/MS	Agricultural workers in Croatia	0.3 to 8.0 μg/g Cr atrazine
[47]	HPLC-ESI-MS	Farmer family in France	9.5 μg/L glyphosate
[48]	LC–MS/MS	Agricultural workers in a rural area from Italy	2.94 μg/L TBA
[21]	ELISA	Farmers from Mexico	0.47 μg/L glyphosate
[49]	MS	Pregnant women from Ghana	0.46 μg/L 2,4-D
[50]	MS	Pregnant women in rural zones of the USA	3.40 ng/mL glyphosate
[51]	HPLC–MS/MS	Amenity horticulturists in Ireland	7.4 μg L^{-1} glyphosate
[52]	ELISA	Farmers in Sri Lanka	0–2.1 mg/g Cr paraquat 48–353 mg/g Cr Glyphosate
[53]	LC-MS/MS	Farmers in the USA	4.04 ppb
[54]	MS/MS	Children and teenagers in Mexico	2.63 μg/mL glyphosate

Table 2.
Analysis studies of herbicides in urine from people living in rural areas.

The monitoring of human groups exposed to chemical agents with the potential to cause damage to the organism is aimed at preserving health and quality of life especially of those populations that are at high risk. Many studies of the exposure of herbicides in agricultural workers exist; one of the most common, biomonitoring, is searching the chemicals in the urine of the people living in agricultural areas. In **Table 2** the most recent studies about the concentrations of herbicides in people from rural areas are shown.

Herbicide exposure is a current problem in public health, especially in developing countries mainly for the following reasons: the main cause of work accidents in agriculture is neglect of safety requirements (28.9%) [55]; workers do not have training for use herbicides and do not use the appropriate personal protective equipment (PPE) for the preparation, application, transportation, and storage [56]. On the other hand, herbicide regulations are less strict or inexistent in developing countries [57], and these chemicals are used by tons because they replace the manual tasks, increasing productive capacity and significantly lowering production costs [10].

6. Damaged environment: How to rehabilitate it?

The use of pesticides to produce food, both to feed local populations and for exportation, should comply with good agricultural practices regardless of the economic status of a country. Farmers should limit the amount of pesticide used to the minimum necessary to protect their crops [5]. One approach is the large-scale implementation of precision agriculture that utilizes remote sensing and responds in real time to crop resource requirements and to weather and climatic conditions. Also, with the cost being such an important factor in consumer choices, policymakers can seek a market-based solution for modifying consumption patterns by better incorporating the true environmental costs to produce a food item [2].

The sustainable rise includes improving agricultural yields while at the same time abating environmental impacts. Relative to scenarios, less-extreme changes toward reducing meat consumption, waste, and the demand for nonfood agricultural products could greatly reduce the environmental impacts of the food system [58]. A few years ago, the agri-environmental scheme (AES) options were rising; these were established as effective strategies to evading contamination peaks when weed burden is high, whereas more demanding AES options guarantee an overall reduction in herbicide use, even during relatively easy farming years in which less weed pressure is experienced [59].

There are several strategies for controlling weeds; one of the practices is the manual weeding that depends on the workforce and is one of the main causes of the loss of organic matter in the soil, due to the excess of weeding and constant plows, making the soil lose its fertility. Therefore, low-income farmers require using herbicides; however, they do so in an uncontrolled manner. These types of practices are not sustainable options for the protection of the environment and occupational health. Moss [60] in his analysis points out that there are approximately 16 reasons why farmers prefer the use of herbicides and within them are economic factors due to the reduction of labor and rapidity of results, in addition to the lack of training and technology among other points.

Numerous studies have provided substantial knowledge to obtain these objectives, noting that one of the strategies is the minimum tillage; however, it is critical and requires effective management, since changes and resistance can be induced in the same herbs, in addition to greater involvement of economists, social scientists, and marketing professionals [12, 60].

In this sense, it is necessary to promote solutions that improve biodiversity and its environment, in addition to maintaining agricultural production; **Figure 1** shows the relationship between the diverse strategies necessary for the sustainable control of weeds.

Farmers are always looking for immediate changes to eliminate weeds; herbicides offer these options, compared to nonchemical strategies that take more time.

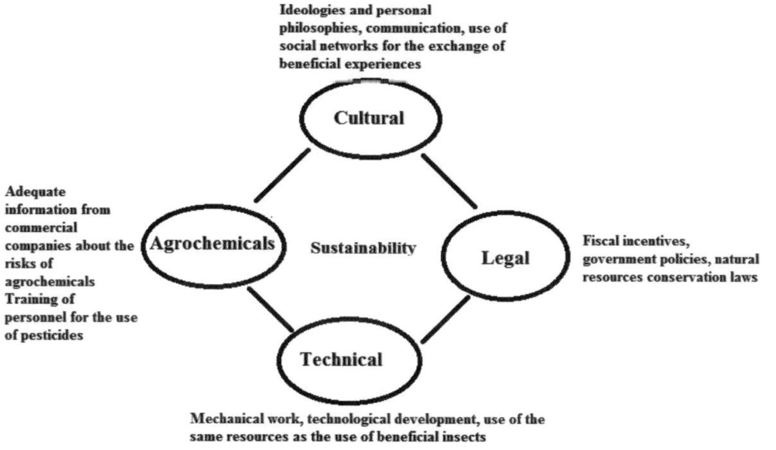

Figure 1.
The main factors that must be involved to achieve sustainable control of the herbs do not benefit the crops.

Some strategies to convince the farmers are to promote crop rotations and field demonstrations, among others, but the most important is to change the farmer mentality which could be achieved by encouraging financial support that could bring about short-term changes [61]; however, attitudinal changes are long-term results that lead to better results.

As was mentioned in Section 3, the global food demand promotes that farmers cannot leave aside the use of herbicides [24]. Consequently, the natural recovery of the soil is not carried out, causing an accumulation of herbicides. This phenomenon is the main factor associated with the development of diseases produced by the chronic exposure of people who work and live in rural areas.

7. Conclusions

The literature analysis indicates that the health problems of agricultural workers are directly related to environmental pollution due to the unsustainable use of herbicides.

Health problems due to the exposure of agricultural workers to herbicides are a major concern, mainly in developing countries. This concern is due to the fact that the use of herbicides in these regions is indiscriminate and the workers have no prior training for their use, so there are no personal protective equipment regulations, and in developing countries there are few or no regulations to address accumulated concentrations in the environment, and there are no regulated biomonitoring in workers.

In rural areas mainly from developing countries, where there are no exists specific standards for their regulations, there is disturbing environmental contamination by herbicides; in these places are reported numerous diseases related to herbicide exposure, which leads to demand in public health services and hence decrease in the workforce, the worker's quality of life, and the growth of the country. That is why herbicide distribution companies should commit to indicate to the users/workers the correct management of the herbicides, including application quantities, as well as, the rigorous use of personal protective equipment.

This research showed that exposure to herbicides by agricultural workers and the environmental contamination with these chemicals are problems that can be solved by enforcing establish regulations in rural zones principally from developing countries.

Acknowledgements

This study was supported by "Programa para el Desarrollo Profesional Docente (PRODEP)," authorization number 511-6/18-8537.

Conflicts of interest

The authors declare no conflict of interest.

Author details

Ana Paola Balderrama-Carmona[1*], Norma Patricia Silva-Beltrán[2], Luis Alberto Zamora Alvarez[1], Norma Patricia Adan Bante[1] and Edgar Felipe Moran Palacio[1]

1 Department of Chemical Biological and Agricultural, Universidad de Sonora, Navojoa, Sonora, Mexico

2 Department of Health Sciences, Universidad de Sonora, Cd. Obregon, Sonora, Mexico

*Address all correspondence to: paola.balderrama@unison.mx

References

[1] Ramankutty N, Mehrabi Z, Waha K, Jarvis L, Kremen C, Herrero M, et al. Trends in global agricultural land use: Implications for environmental health and food security. Annual Review of Plant Biology. 2018;**69**:789-815. DOI: 10.1146/annurev-arplant-042817-040256

[2] Davis KF, Gephart JA, Emery KA, Leach AM, Galloway JN, D'Odorico P. Meeting future food demand with current agricultural resources. Global Environmental Change. 2016;**39**:12-132. DOI: 10.1016/j.gloenvcha.2016.05.004

[3] Kim KH, Kabir E, Jahan SA. Exposure to pesticides and the associated human health effects. The Science of the Total Environment. 2017;**575**:525-535. DOI: 10.1016/j.scitotenv.2016.09.009

[4] Sankhla MS, Kumari M, Sharma K, Kushwah RS, Kumar R. Water contamination through pesticide & their toxic effect on human health. International Journal for Research in Applied Science & Engineering Technology. 2018;**6**:867-970

[5] Landrigan PJ, Fuller R, Acosta NJR, Adeyi O, Arnold R, Basu N, et al. The lancet commission on pollution and health. The Lancet. 2017;**391**:462-512. DOI: 10.1016/S0140-6736(17)32345-0

[6] WHO Pesticide residues in food [Internet]. 2018. Available from: https://www.who.int/news-room/fact-sheets/detail/pesticide-residues-in-food

[7] Landrigan PJ, Benbrook C. GMOs, herbicides, and public health. The New England Journal of Medicine. 2015;**373**:693-695. DOI: 10.1056/NEJMp150566

[8] Tarone RE. On the international agency for research on cancer classification of glyphosate as a probable human carcinogen. European Journal of Cancer Prevention. 2018;**27**(1):82-87. DOI: 10.1097/CEJ.0000000000000289

[9] Rubio F, Guo E, Kamp L. Survey of glyphosate residues in honey, corn and soy products. Journal of Environmental & Analytical Toxicology. 2014;**5**:1. DOI: 10.4172/2161-0525.1000249

[10] Haggblade S, Minten B, Pray C, Reardon T, Zilberman D. The herbicide revolution in developing countries: Patterns, causes, and implications. The European Journal of Development Research. 2017;**29**:533-559. DOI: 10.1057/s41287-017-0090-7

[11] Kesavachandran C, Pathak MK, Fareed M, Bihari V, Mathur N, Srivastava AK. Health risks of employees working in pesticide retail shops: An exploratory study. Indian Journal of Occupational and Environment Medicine. 2009;**13**(3):121-126. DOI: 10.4103/0019-5278.58914

[12] Food and Agriculture Organization (FAO). The State of Food and Agriculture: Leveraging Food Systems for Inclusive Rural Transformation. Rome, Italy: Food and Agriculture Organization of the United Nations; 2017, ISBN 978-92-5-109873-8. Available from: http://www.fao.org/3/a-I7658e.pdf [Accessed: July 2019]

[13] Sims S, Corsi S, Gbehounou G, Kienzle J, Taguchi M, Friedrich T. Sustainable weed management for conservation agriculture: Options for smallholder farmers. Agriculture. 2018;**8**:118. DOI: 10.3390/agriculture8080000

[14] Sidoli P, Baran N, Angulo-Jaramillo R. Glyphosate and AMPA adsorption in soils: Laboratory experiments and pedotransfer rules. Environmental Science and Pollutution Research. 2016;**23**:5733-5742

[15] Baumgartner D, Godoy de Souza E, Renata Machado SC, Furlan MM. Correlation between 2,4-D herbicide residues and soil attributes in southern of Brazil. Revista Ciência Agronômica. 2017;**48**:428-437

[16] Scherr KE, Bielsk L, Kosubov P, Dinisov P, Hvezdov M, Hofman ZJ. Occurrence of chlorotriazine herbicides and their transformation products in arable soils. Environmental Pollution. 2017;**222**:283-293

[17] Sapcanin A, Cakal M, Imamovic B, Salihovic M, Pehlic E, Jacimovic Z, et al. Herbicide and pesticide occurrence in the soils of children's playgrounds in Sarajevo, Bosnia and Herzegovina. Environmental Monitoring and Assessment. 2016;**188**:450. DOI: 10.1007/s10661-016-5463-4

[18] Leyva-soto LA, Balderrama-Carmona AP, Moran-Palacio EF, Díaz-Tenorio LM, Gortares-Moroyoqui P. Glyphosate and aminomethylphosphonic acid in population of agricultural fields: Health risk assessment overview. Applied Ecology and Environmental Research. 2018;**16**(4):5127-5140. DOI: 10.15666/aeer/1604_51275140

[19] Mahler BJ, Van Metre PC, Burley TE, Loftin KA, Meyer MT, Nowell LH. Similarities and differences in occurrence and temporal fluctuations in glyphosate and atrazine in small Midwestern streams (USA) during the 2013 growing season. The Science of the Total Environment. 2017;**579**:149-158

[20] Almberg KS, Turyk ME, Jones RM, Rankin K, Freels S, Stayner LS. Atrazine contamination of drinking water and adverse birth outcomes in community water systems with elevated atrazine in Ohio, 2006-2008. International Journal of Environmental Research and Public Health. 2018;**15**:1889. DOI: 10.3390/ijerph15091889

[21] Rendón-von Osten J, Dzul-Caamal R. Glyphosate residues in groundwater, drinking water and urine of subsistence farmers from intensive agriculture localities: A survey in Hopelchén, Campeche, Mexico. International Journal of Environmental Research and Public Health. 2017;**14**:595. DOI: 10.3390/ijerph14060595

[22] Li Z, Jennings A. Worldwide regulations of standard values of pesticides for human health risk control: A review. International Journal of Environmental Research and Public Health. 2017;**14**:826. DOI: 10.3390/ijerph14070826

[23] Khare S. Pesticide contamination in India and its health effects. International Journal of Scientific and Technical Research in Engineering. 2018;**3**:8-14. Available from: http://www.ijstre.com/Publish/342018/189099991.pdf

[24] Fuhrimann S, Winkler MS, Staudacher P, Weiss FT, Stamm C, Eggen RI, et al. Exposure to pesticides and health effects on farm owners and workers from conventional and organic agricultural farms in Costa Rica: Protocol for a cross-sectional study. JMIR Research Protocols. 2019;**8**(1):e10914. DOI: 10.2196/10914

[25] Kori RK, Sing MK, Jain AK, Yadav RS. Neurochemical and behavioral dysfunctions in pesticide exposed farm workers: A clinical outcome. Indian Journal of Clinical Biochemistry. 2018;**33**:372-381. DOI: 10.1007/s12291-018-0791-5

[26] Negatu B, Vermeulen R, Mekonnen Y, Kromhout H. Neurobehavioural symptoms and acute pesticide poisoning: A cross-sectional study among male pesticide applicators selected from three commercial farming systems in Ethiopia. Occupational and Environmental Medicine. 2018;**75**:283-289. DOI: 10.1136/oemed-2017-104538

[27] Klingelschmidt J, Milner A, Khireddine-Medouni I, Witt K, Alexopoulos EC, Toivanen S, et al. Suicide among agricultural, forestry, and fishery workers: A systematic literature review and meta-analysis. Scandinavian Journal of Work, Environment & Health. 2018;**44**(1):3-15. DOI: 10.5271/sjweh.3682

[28] Androutsopoulos VP, Hernandez AF, Liesivuori J, Tsatsakis AM. A mechanistic overview of health associated effects of low levels of organochlorine and organophosphorous pesticides. Toxicology. 2013;**307**:89-94. DOI: 10.1016/j.tox.2012.09.011

[29] Chin-Chan M, Navarro-Yepes J, Quintanilla-Vega B. Environmental pollutants as risk factors for neurodegenerative disorders: Alzheimer and Parkinson diseases. Environmental pollutants as risk factors for neurodegenerative disorders: Alzheimer and Parkinson diseases. Frontiers of Cellular Neuroscience. 2015;**9**:124. DOI: 10.3389/fncel.2015.00124

[30] Bastías-Candia S, Zolezzi JM, Inestrosa NC. Revisiting the paraquat-induced sporadic Parkinson's disease-like model. Molecular Neurobiology. 2019;**56**:1044-1055. DOI: 10.1007/s12035-018-1148-z

[31] Martenies SE, Perry MJ. Environmental and occupational pesticide exposure and human sperm parameters: A systematic review. Toxicology. 2013;**3017**:66-73. DOI: 10.1016/j.tox.2013.02.005

[32] Pellegriti G, Frasca F, Regalbuto C, Squatrito S, Vigneri R. Worldwide increasing incidence of thyroid cancer: Update on epidemiology and risk factors. Journal of Cancer Epidemiology. 2013;**2013**:965212. DOI: 10.1155/2013/965212

[33] Buralli RJ, Ribeiro H, Mauad T, Amato-Lourenço LF, Salge JM, Diaz-Quijano FA, et al. Respiratory condition of family farmers exposed to pesticides in the state of Rio de Janeiro, Brazil. International Journal of Environmental Research and Public Health. 2018;**15**:1203. DOI: 10.3390/ijerph15061203

[34] Hoppin JA, Umbach DM, Long S, London SJ, Henneberger PK, Blair A, et al. Pesticides are associated with allergic and non-allergic wheeze among male farmers. Environmental Health Perspectives. 2017;**125**:535-543. DOI: 10.1289/EHP315

[35] Halliwell B. Oxygen and nitrogen are pro-carcinogens. Damage to DNA by reactive oxygen, chlorine and nitrogen species: Measurement, mechanism and the effects of nutrition. Mutation Research, Genetic Toxicology and Environmental Mutagenesis. 1999;**443**:37-52. DOI: 10.1016/S1383-5742(99)00009-5

[36] Simoniello MF, Kleinsorge EC, Scagnetti JA, Mastandrea C, Grigolato RA, Paonessa AM, et al. Biomarkers of cellular reaction to pesticide exposure in a rural population. Biomarkers. 2010;**15**(1):5260. DOI: 10.3109/13547500903276378

[37] Casals-Casas C, Desvergne B. Endocrine disruptors: From endocrine to metabolic disruption. Annual Review of Physiology. 2011;**73**:135-162. DOI: 10.1146/annurev-physiol-012110-142200

[38] Lee K, Park EK, Stoecklin-Marois M. Occupational paraquat exposure of agricultural workers in large costa Rican farms. International Archives of Occupational and Environmental Health. 2009;**82**:455. DOI: 10.1007/s00420-008-0356-7

[39] Gore AC, Chappell VA, Fenton SE, Flaws JA, Nadal A, Prins GS, et al. EDC-2: The endocrine society's second scientific statement on

endocrine-disrupting chemicals. Endocrine Reviews. 2015;**36**:E1-E150. DOI: 10.1210/er.2015-1010

[40] Ramírez-Santana M, Iglesias-Guerrero J, Castillo-Riquelme M, Scheepers PTJ. Assessment of health care and economic costs due to episodes of acute pesticide intoxication in workers of rural areas of the Coquimbo region, Chile. Value in Health Regional Issues. 2014;**5**:35-39. DOI: 10.1016/j.vhri.2014.07.006

[41] Buendía JA, Restrepo-Chavarriaga GJ. Costo de la intoxicación por paraquat en Colombia. Value in Health Regional Issues. 2019;**20**:110-114. DOI: 10.1016/j.vhri.2019.02.006

[42] OECD. How's life? [Internet]. 2017. Available from: http://www.oecdbetterlifeindex.org/

[43] Cely-Andrade JL, Garcia-Ubaque JC, Manrique-Abril F. Quality of life related to health in the mining population of Boyacá. Revista de Salud Pública. 2017;**19**(3):362-367. DOI: 10.15446/rsap.v19n3.56163

[44] Panuwet P, Prapamontol T, Chantara S, Barr DB. Urinary pesticide metabolites in school students from northern Thailand. International Journal of Hygiene and Environmental Health. 2009;**212**:288-297. DOI: 10.1016/j.ijheh.2008.07.002

[45] Rodríguez T, van Wendel de Joode B, Lindh CH, et al. Assessment of long-term and recent pesticide exposure among rural school children in Nicaragua. Occupational and Environmental Medicine. 2012;**69**:119-125. DOI: 10.1136/oem.2010.062539

[46] Mendaš G, Vuletić M, Galić N, Drevenkar V. Urinary metabolites as biomarkers of human exposure to atrazine: Atrazine mercapturate in agricultural workers. Toxicology Letters. 2012;**210**:174-181. DOI: 10.1016/j.toxlet.2011.11.023

[47] Mesnage R, Moesch C, Le Grand R, Lauthier G, de Vendomois JS, Gress S, et al. Glyphosate exposure in a farmer's family. BioMed Research International. 2014;**1**:1-8. DOI: 10.1155/2014/179691

[48] Mercadante R, Polledri E, Bertazzi PA, Fustinoni S. Biomonitoring short- and long-term exposure to the herbicide terbuthylazine in agriculture workers and in the general population using urine and hair specimens. Environment International. 2013;**60**:42-47. DOI: 10.1016/j.envint.2013.07.016

[49] Wylie BJ, Ae-Ngibise KA, Boamah EA, Mujtaba M, Messerlian C, Hauser R, et al. Urinary concentrations of insecticide and herbicide metabolites among pregnant women in rural Ghana: A pilot study. International Journal of Environmental Research and Public Health. 2017;**14**(4):354. DOI: 10.3390/ijerph14040354

[50] Parvez S, Gerona RR, Proctor C, Friesen M, Ashby JL, Reiter JL, et al. Glyphosate exposure in pregnancy and shortened gestational length: A prospective Indiana birth cohort study. Environmental Health. 2018;**17**:23. DOI: 10.1186/s12940-018-0367-0

[51] Connolly A, Jones K, Basinas I, Galea KS, Kenny L, McGowan P, et al. Exploring the half-life of glyphosate in human urine samples. International Journal of Hygiene and Environmental Health. 2019;**222**:205-210. DOI: 10.1016/j.ijheh.2018.09.004

[52] De Silva PMC, Abdul K, Jayasinghe S, Chandana S, Jayasumana C, Siribaddana S. Occupational herbicide exposure and declining kidney functions among sugarcane farmers In rural Sri Lanka. Kidney International Reports. 2019;**4**:S102-S103. DOI: 10.1016/j.ekir.2019.05.265

[53] Perry MJ, Mandrioli D, Belpoggi F, Manservisi F, Panzacchi S, Irwin C. Historical evidence of glyphosate exposure from a US agricultural cohort. Environmental Health. 2019;**18**:42. DOI: 10.1186/s12940-019-0474-6

[54] Sierra-Diaz E, Celis-de la Rosa AJ, Lozano-Kasten F, Trasande L, Peregrina-Lucano AA, Sandoval-Pinto E, et al. Urinary pesticide levels in children and adolescents residing in two agricultural communities in Mexico. International Journal of Environmental Research and Public Health. 2019;**16**(4):562. DOI: 10.3390/ijerph16040562

[55] Enn A, Merisalu E. Causes and consequences of work accidents in Estonian agriculture. Occupational and Environmental Medicine. 2019;**76**:P.3.10. DOI: 10.1136/OEM-2019-EPI.271

[56] Andrade-Rivas F, Rothe HA. Chemical exposure reduction: Factors impacting on south African herbicide sprayers' personal protective equipment compliance and highrisk work practices. Environmental Research. 2015;**142**:34-45. DOI: 10.1016/j.envres.2015.05.028

[57] Zomorrodi A, Zhou X. Role of EKC and PHH in determining environment quality and their relation to economic growth of a country. Asian Journal of Economics and Empirical Research. 2016;**3**(2):139-144. DOI: 10.20448/journal.501/2016.3.2/501.2.139.144

[58] Poore J, Nemecek T. Reducing food's environmental impacts through producers and consumers. Science. 2019;**360**:987-992. DOI: 10.1126/science.aaw9908

[59] Brethour C, Weersink A. An economic evaluation of the environmental benefits from pesticide reduction. Agricultural Economics. 2001;**25**:219-226. DOI: 10.1111/j.1574-0862. 2001.tb00202.x

[60] Moss S. Integrated weed management (IWM): Why are farmers reluctant to adopt non-chemical alternatives to herbicides. Pest Management Science. 2019;**75**:1205-1211. DOI: 10.1002/ps.5267

[61] Jussaume RA, Ervin D. Understanding weed resistance as a wicked problem to improve weed management decisions. Weed Science. 2016;**64**:559-569. DOI: 10.1614/WS-D-15-00131.1

Section 2

Case Studies

Chapter 5

Governance for Sustainable Remediation of Polluted Soil in Developing Countries

Henrik Haller, Ginnette Flores-Carmenate and Anders Jonsson

Abstract

Environmental governance is a challenge for many developing countries, and soil pollution is typically overlooked by authorities in the Global South. Soil governance should protect people and environment from the hazards of pollution and promote sustainable remediation of polluted sites through legislation and soil policies that facilitate the use of appropriate technology. Today, however, the soil governance landscape is highly fragmented and often fails to adequately address these concerns. Combining soil remediation with profitable activities (alone or in combination) such as food and fiber production, biomass energy production, erosion control, carbon sequestration, favoring biodiversity, etc. is potentially an appropriate strategy to promote the decontamination of polluted agriculture soil in low-income countries. Many potential pitfalls follow such a strategy but decision support tools may provide insights from the latest scientific remediation findings to stakeholders in their exploration of policy options. This chapter explores challenges and opportunities for sustainable soil governance in developing countries.

Keywords: soil governance, developing countries, soil pollution, bioremediation, DPSIR, phytoremediation

1. Introduction

Soil pollution i.e. presence in soil of substances out of place and/or present at higher than normal concentrations that has adverse effects on non-targeted organism, is a serious threat to food security and human health in developing countries [1–5]. At least one third of the world's ecosystems are currently suffering from different effects of pollution [6]. The exact scale of global soil pollution is unknown but according to some estimations, at least 22 million hectares may be affected globally [7]. Rodríguez-Eugenio et al. [4] argue that this number probably underestimates the scale of the problem. Due to insufficient data about the scale and implications of the problem, soil pollution is sometimes referred to as a hidden reality that is largely invisible to the international community [4, 8].

In developing countries, the magnitude of the soil pollution is largely an uncharted territory with limited knowledge of the extension and location of soil pollution hotspots. Soil pollution in developing countries comes from a number of sources. Often these are derived from anthropogenic processes, but also geogenic sources such as weathering and volcanic eruptions can be as important as anthropogenic sources in terms of risks to human health [9–11]. Large-scale application of persistent pesticides is one prominent source of pollution in developing countries, that has affected large areas of land historically [1, 3, 12] and in most countries in the Global South, inadequate applications of pesticides is an ongoing process that continues to pollute large areas of soil.

Soil pollution causes significant losses of income, as well as impacts on food security and direct hazards to human health. Typically, different groups of people are affected unequally by soil pollution. For instance, nutritionally marginal persons and women who tend to have higher percentages of body fat may carry more lipophilic pesticides and heavy metals which expose them to greater risks [13, 14]. Soil contaminants can enter the human body via three main routes: eating, inhalation, and dermal absorption. The exposure through *eating* can either happen indirectly by eating plants grown on contaminated soil, which are subsequently consumed by humans or by agricultural livestock or by direct ingestion of the soil (geophagia). Particularly, children under 3 years of age are susceptible to this kind of exposure that is one important pathway for human exposure to soil contamination. *Inhalation* and *dermal absorption* (through skin contact) is primarily a problem for agriculture workers who handle pesticides and a pathway from previously contaminated soil to humans [15, 16].

Among the different challenges that developing countries face, soil pollution is typically assigned low priority and is thus often overlooked by authorities in the Global South [13, 17–19]. Although progress has been made to strengthen the legal and regulatory frameworks during the last decades, poor environmental governance is still common in low and middle income countries and monitoring and enforcement of environmental regulations remains a challenge [20]. At the same time, experiences from remediation programs have shown that the complexity and cost of remediation and restoration tend to grow with time. Not only are the societal costs of inaction great but potential benefits (in terms of increased health, property values, poverty reduction etc.) from remediation projects may be substantial [20]. However, since those benefits tend to be collective rather than benefitting individual landowners or liable persons, even cheaper and less resource-intense remediation methods are often not perceived as lucrative, at least not as stand-alone technologies. In order to materialize, in developing countries, remediation projects on private or cooperative-owned land thus needs that the persons in charge of the polluted area perceive a strong, direct economic incentive from remediating the land [17, 18].

The need for innovative solutions to remediate the growing number of polluted fields in developing countries is increasingly urgent since the number of polluted sites that require remediation doubles every 25 years [21]. Many farmers in developing countries presently operate on polluted land, and the scarcity of agriculture land will inevitably force more farmers to cultivate food in contaminated areas as the human population increases [22]. A number of remediation technologies for polluted soil exist, ranging from expensive and resource-intense ex-situ technologies to slower and more cost-effective solutions that tend to be gentler on the ecosystems such as *natural attenuation*. Many of the conventional energy-intense solutions are unaffordable for most sites in developing countries except for some urban sites where the high land value would motivate the additional cost for a speedy solution. In areas of little economic value such as most rural areas in developing countries, the high costs involved in removal of toxic substances from polluted soils often prevent remediation from being carried out [23]. Often, time constraints are not as limiting as in industrialized contexts since alternative remediation options are typically non-existing. In addition to being profitable and provide perceptible and achievable benefits, soil remediation solutions for developing countries need to be cost-effective and compatible with the social and economic development state of the region.

One way to make remediation projects appealing in developing countries is to integrate the remediation project with value-adding measures such as production of energy crops, food production, erosion control, and carbon sequestration. Multifunctional production system that yield biomass for fuel, fiber, or safe food crops at the same as they remediate polluted soils and sequester carbon are potentially very appropriate methods in this context. Although such strategies may be appropriate options for most pollutants, a number of challenges and potential pitfalls need to be surmounted. Challenges may be associated with the application of the remediation technology since projects need to be tailor-made for the specific site they address. Commercial one-fits-all solutions can typically not address the heterogeneity and complex (socio-economic, cultural, and environmental) contexts of most polluted sites in developing countries. Other challenges are related to inadequate soil governance (such as inefficient laws, lack of policy and law enforcement) that may hamper the execution of appropriate soil remediation projects. The aim of this chapter is to explore governance and socio-institutional limitations and opportunities for development of appropriate soil remediation technology for developing countries.

2. Technology transitions

Technologies for soil remediation in developing countries need to meet a different set of criteria than in sites of high land value in industrialized countries in order to be adopted. First, polluted sites in developing countries are accorded less attention by authorities and investors compared to polluted sites in industrialized countries [24–28]. Furthermore, a great fraction of the inhabitants in developing countries are systematically denied full access to many opportunities, resources, and rights and prevented from participating fully in the economic, social, and political life of the society, which makes them marginalized and vulnerable to technological mismatches and unsustainable technology transfer [28].

The transition toward a sustainable society needs behavioral changes as well as implementation of new technologies. New technologies, improvements and adaptation of current technologies are crucial but the socio-institutional sustainability related to such technology transfers is often neglected when implemented in developing countries [29]. Sustainability transition analysis based on theories such as multi-level perspective or strategic niche management, often lead to a focus on increased resource efficiency but ignoring the risk that poverty creating structures are reproduced from one state to another in such transitions even if the resource turnover rate is decreased [30, 31]. In the Global South where technological, cultural and social needs differ fundamentally from the Global North, the lack of understanding of these mechanisms and the assumption that all problems of resource governance can be represented by a small set of simple models [32] often lead to technological and cultural mismatches when regional capabilities, objectives and benefits are neglected or expressed in unrealistic terms [12, 33]. Over-reliance on technological fixes in developing countries where access to technology is often limited may further add to this problem. Sustainability challenges such as soil pollution are by definition multidisciplinary and need a broad array of methodological tools to be disentangled. The failure to include views from pertinent scientific fields and political, cultural, and institutional dynamics in sustainability assessments tends to lead to misinterpretations and overlooking issues that are outside the scope of the expertise in the project groups.

Multidisciplinary visions are thus needed when analyzing different remediation options favoring the ones that contribute to catalyze the transition toward environmental, cultural, and socio-institutional sustainability. Conventional approaches to soil remediation typically focus on the internalities of a remediation project (effectiveness of the remedy, implementability, cost considerations, time constraints, etc.) [34]. The environmental viability of specific remediation technologies has traditionally received little attention from researchers, let alone the social aspects of remediation projects.

In order to be sustainable in developing countries, remediation methods need to be suited to the immediate socio-economic, cultural and environment contexts in which they are introduced [35]. One discipline that attempts to promote a technological transfer that address the issues of poverty, social equity, gender equality and basic human needs is the concept of *appropriate technology.* The grassroots appropriate technology movement had its peak during the 1970s and although the number of NGOs dedicated to the promotion of appropriate technology decreased during the following decades, the movement has not lost its momentum. Initially, advocates of appropriate technology prescribed solutions that should be small-scale, labor-intensive, low capital investment per worker, energy efficient, environmentally sound and controlled and maintained by the local community [36–39]. However, many theorists such as Ranis [40] argue that appropriate technology can also be advanced, modern, capital intensive, etc. depending on the available resources, local preferences, time, and place. In developing countries, soil pollution is found in rural areas as well as in relatively wealthy areas with high land values in urbanized areas, and the most appropriate remediation technology may look very different depending on the context. With a definition such as Ranis's, appropriate soil remediation technology should seek to maximize the society's objectives given that society's capabilities rather than categorically favoring low tech, small scale solution.

3. Governance instruments for sustainable soil remediation in developing countries

The design of soil remediation projects, no matter how appropriate they are, needs to be implemented to be able to reduce pollution. A significant risk in developing countries is that inadequate soil governance may hamper its implementation or impede remediation projects from materializing altogether. Soil governance may be defined as the network of formal and informal institutions (e.g. legal prescriptions, regulations, market incentives, rules, norms, habits, and attitudes) that concern soil-related decision-making processes of state and non-state actors at different decision-making levels [41]. The ultimate goal of governance for sustainable remediation of polluted soil is to protect people and environment from the hazards of pollution and promote sustainable remediation of polluted sites through legislation and soil policies and manage conflicts between stakeholders about soil [42, 43].

Despite attempts to unify soil governance efforts internationally by the Food and Agriculture Organization of the United Nations (FAO) who have established the Global Soil Partnership (GSP) [44], the soil governance landscape is still highly fragmented and soil and water pollution management policies are often not integrated with food safety policies [41, 45]. Even in the most stringently regulated countries, legislation applicable to soil pollution and food security often lags behind state-of-the-art, and in developing countries, this discrepancy is particularly palpable [45, 46]. As a result of this, legislation and policies often fail to adequately address problems related to soil pollution and food security [43, 45, 46].

3.1 Legislation

Legal frameworks and the implementation of these differ substantially between countries but in most low and middle income countries, regulation instruments are insufficient to address soil pollution [1, 43], and the lack of the enforcement of environmental laws leads to that huge polluted areas with unknown concentrations of numerous pollutants are used for agriculture, recreation or construction. The polluter-pays principle is a fundamental legislative principle that is enacted to make the party responsible for producing pollution responsible for paying for the damage done to the environment. A variation of the polluter-pays principle exists that has been adopted by a number of developing countries, including India, Malaysia, Taiwan, Ecuador, Chile, Costa Rica, Kenya, South Africa, and among others, where the government instead is directly responsible for payment and environmental monitoring. According to an assessment of the two strategies, government-pays regimes may be preferable in situations characterized by widespread poverty, high interest rates and judicial delays and uncertainty—however, there is a risk that local governments choose a level of monitoring that minimizes the financial exposure of the local government but does not fully internalize the costs as well as the benefits of the agents' care [47].

To date, many developing countries lack specific laws on soil pollution prevention and management [4, 8]. Until 2018, there was no specific law governing soil pollution in China but a soil pollution action plan based on the law, with regulations, risk control rules, and technical guidelines developed by the Ministry of Environment and Ecology had a similar role. In August 2018, the Soil Pollution Prevention and Control Law was adopted as the first specialized law on soil pollution prevention in China. The law stipulates principles, measures, and goals of soil management and essentially adopts a protection-first and polluter-pays approach [48].

Two major legislative strategies are used to protect people from exposure to pollutants: maximum permissible concentrations (MPC) and different risk-based approaches and both strategies have their limitations in terms of protecting people from exposure to pollution. Limitations with MPC legislation include insufficient number of regulated pollutants [49] and concentrations that do not respond to up-to-date knowledge about toxicity [50]. MPCs are also largely limited to metals and thresholds of soil contamination by organochlorine pollutants are typically not available for agricultural use of the soil [51], and many developing countries have not developed their own MPCs but follow MPCs from other countries whose context may not be applicable. Critiques of risk-based approaches argue that although they can offer important benefits, they also face a range of epistemic, institutional, and normative challenges [52], which may be unsurmountable for administrations in developing countries that are already under considerable pressure.

3.2 Policies and standards

Development of policies for soil pollution and remediation in developing countries is a complex process that must consider not only the legal requirements but also technical practicability, scientific knowledge, economic, and cultural aspects, thus implying an intensive consultation of a high number of actors [44]. Since the 1970s, environmental policies have evolved from the prevention of local pollution to a more holistic management of the natural resources [53], but currently there is no global soil framework that has the agreement of national governments, and soil governance thus follows a fragmented structure from global policy documents and agreements to local attitudes and customs [44]. Since there is no global thematic strategy on soil protection, less all-encompassing standards and policies may be used, to prevent people from exposure to contaminated soil. There is a remarkable scarcity when it comes to international standards and guidelines to avoid exposure to soil pollution and the ones that exist commonly focus on food security or food production [4, 8]. The Codex Alimentarius, for example, is one such collection of internationally recognized standards, codes of practice, guidelines, and other recommendations relative to food production, and food safety that may fill some of the void and offer guidelines for soil pollution problems that are related to food production. The Codex Alimentarius provides guidelines for maximum concentrations of a substance based on WHOs maximum monthly intake that can be legally permitted in a commodity (food or feed) for a number of substances.

Good Agricultural Practices (GAP) is another collection of principles that applies to on-farm production processes as well as post-production processes to achieve safe and healthy food and non-food agricultural products. GAP uses a holistic perspective and training manuals on implementation of GAP typically include a number of aspects that are relevant to avoid exposure to polluted soil. Modules from such manuals include topics such as site history and management to identify risk of contamination from previous use of chemically or biologically hazardous substances, current use of fertilizers and soil additives [54]. Importing countries as well as domestic buyers can require producers to implement GAP, which may support the diffusion of the standard.

3.3 Decision support tools

Decision support tools are designed to support different stakeholders in the exploration of policy options in participatory processes by facilitating dialog and exchange of information. Such tools may have an important niche to fill in developing countries where legislation and policy may be deficient to provide insights from the latest scientific bioremediation findings to non-expert decision makers. For example, knowledge on bioaccumulation patterns of plants grown in a certain area could help regulators or change agents to emit informed recommendations on sound agriculture practices including species and cultivation protocols that are known to produce food with safe levels of pollutants. A number of attempts have been made to support decision makers with guidelines when designing sustainable remediation project in various contexts in developing countries by Haller et al. [17], Tang et al. [22], Clostre et al. [51], and others. In a critical review on decision-support tools for assessment of sites in need of remediation, Huysegoms and Cappuyns [55] conclude that the selection of alternatives is often inappropriate and that there is typically a disparity favoring the environmental aspect compared to economic and social aspects. Although social aspects such as human health and safety receives a considerable amount of attention but ethics and equity are seldom considered.

4. The *Driver-Pressure-State-Impact-Response* (DPSIR) framework for soil governance

The complexity of large-scale remediation projects in developing countries may seem like an overwhelming task to many actors. Employees at municipalities and county boards, NGOs, contractors, and consultants involved in remediation projects may benefit from frameworks such as DPSIR to structure particular environmental problems and identify appropriate responses

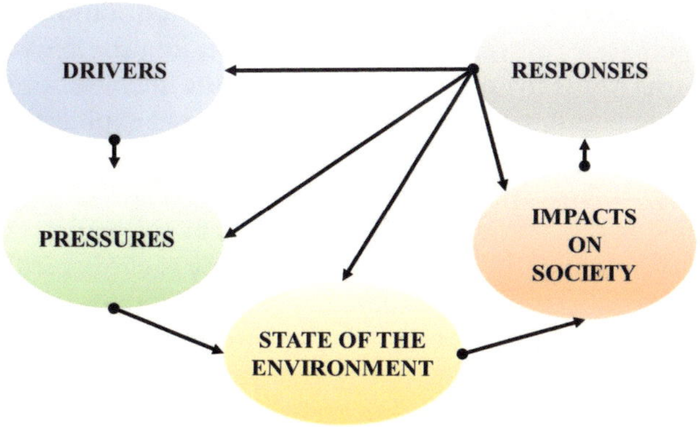

Figure 1.
A visual representation of the constituents and flows of DPSIR framework.

(**Figure 1**) [17]. DPSIR departs from the idea that there is a chain of causal links going from *driving forces* (fundamental social processes such as economic sectors, human activities, etc.) through *pressures* (human activities with impact on the environment), (environmental) *states*, *impacts* on ecosystems, human health, and functions to *responses* by policy-makers [56–60]. The DPSIR model has gained attention by researchers and policy-makers because of its multidisciplinary nature, its simplified, yet structured, methodological applicability in a number of environmental issues, its capacity to provide an overview of the problem in question and to identify policy options and solutions through the selection and monitoring of indicators and objectives or goals within each category of the model [60, 61]. Today, the DSPIR framework is a central component of Integrated Environmental Assessment, and it has been adopted as a strategy for United Nations Environment Programme (UNEP) among others [57, 58, 62–64]. The outcomes of a DPSIR analysis may be useful to narrow the communication gap among the scientific, political, and public spheres about soil governance issues, which makes this tool attractive for policy-making purposes. In Section 4.1, a case study from agricultural region Chinandega in Nicaragua illustrates how DSPIR can be used to structure environmental problems related to soil pollution in a developing country and to generate ideas on how to design soil remediation projects that are compatible with sustainable development in an economically vulnerable region.

4.1 Chinandega, Nicaragua—a case study of DPSIR application for soil governance

The region of Chinandega in Nicaragua is characterized by lack of financial power, low income, poorly implemented regulations, lack of public information about the pollution, etc. that often leave private farmers with no other alternatives than to grow their food in the polluted soils previously used for cotton cultivation [17, 65–68]. The DPSIR framework was used to describe the chain of causal links that define the soil pollution situation in the Chinandega region and identify interrelating cause-effect connections among the economic, social, and natural systems that are demanding soil remediation solutions. The analysis aspires to provide structured information that can improve the understanding of the scope of the problem and facilitate the identification of opportunities and limitations for implementing sustainable soil remediation initiatives in Chinandega.

Figure 2 shows a DPSIR scheme for the soil pollution situation in Chinandega. Given that Chinandega is primarily an agricultural region, the *driving forces* are characterized by the needs for agricultural food supply, income, and labor, coupled to a positive trend in population growth. Despite high per capita natural resources, Nicaragua is the second poorest nation in Central America and the agricultural workers are among the lowest paid in the country [66]. The lack of political willingness and the lack of awareness about the severity of the soil pollution issue among producers (local farmers) and their consumers are key socio-institutional *drivers* that aggravate the problem and perpetuate the lack of alternatives [17].

These *drivers* trigger a generalized poor management of the soils (i.e., *pressures*) with the excessive use of mineral fertilizers and chemical pesticides, inappropriate crop cultivation techniques, unsuitable livestock farming practices, etc. and altogether contribute to soil erosion, loss of soil fertility, and pesticides pollution. Land-use changes are also part of the *pressures* generated from the *drivers* above [69]. When the soil becomes severely degraded, farmers are forced to abandon the land and conquer new agriculture sites through deforestation [69]. The *pressure* of climate change arises from numerous global socio-economic *drivers*, and it is a source of many pressures on the environment itself. It also compromises the integrity of the less resilient socio-ecological systems at all scales all over the world [70]. In poor and rural areas like Chinandega, agricultural production, water resources, human health, and ecosystems are greatly affected by a changing local climate, all which increases considerably the vulnerability of the region and aggravates the situation by intensifying the magnitude of the pressures exerted on those systems. *Pressures* coming from the excessive use of mineral fertilizers and organochlorine/organophosphorus pesticides in the past can be categorized as *past pressures*; however, they continue to have an impact on the present *state* of the environment [17].

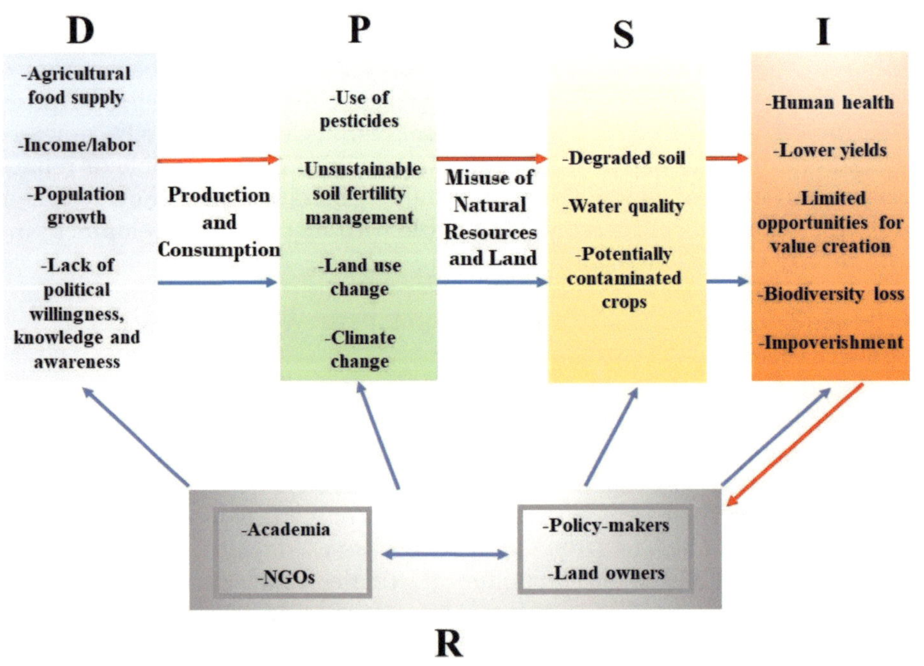

Figure 2.
Application of the DPSIR model in the context of Chinandega. Red arrows indicate the current situation and non-desired relations. Blue arrows indicate relations that are needed to promote a sustainable management of the soil resources in Chinandega.

The outcome of these *pressures* is a degraded and severely polluted soil (i.e., *state*). The degradation affects also the water quality of lagoons and reservoirs through the run-off and leaching from the polluted soils and potentially affects the quality of the agricultural production because of the uptake and translocation of the soil contaminants to the edible parts of the plants. As a result, this environmental *state* of the soils *impacts* the local and regional biodiversity because of the effects on the ecosystems (e.g., perturbation of trophic chains and the biotic phase of the soils, contamination of water sources, resistance to pesticides, phytotoxicity, etc.). The human health is also *impacted* by the local consumption of contaminated agricultural products and contaminated drinking water supply. The occupational safety and health of farmers that employ agrochemicals like pesticides and chemical fertilizers is also jeopardized [65, 68, 69]. Furthermore, because of the present pollution the land might suffer from economic devaluation which in turn could discourage greater investments to support, for example, soil remediation costs or more sustainable soil management practices. Lands being either over- or underused is a condition that is affecting not only Chinandega but all the agricultural regions in Nicaragua [66] and many other agricultural regions in developing countries. This condition reduces the capacity to take full advantage of the potential of the agricultural production which impedes the development of important market niches in the agricultural sector and also the mitigation of poverty in economically important rural regions like Chinandega. However, if the soil contamination problem is not addressed, farmers may find difficulties to export their agricultural produce because it might not meet international safety standards. The vast majority of the population in Chinandega relies on agricultural production as their principal means of support and farmers are thus the most affected social group by the *impacts* of the contaminated and degraded lands of the region. Obsolete and unsustainable agricultural technologies and practices and underpaid agricultural workers are some of the most important causes of impoverishment in Chinandega rural communities.

Nicaragua essentially lacks legislation that regulates the soil use except for some dispersed and not compulsory norms. Policy actions (i.e., *responses*) that address the soil degradation problem in the region of Chinandega are virtually non-existent. Lack of knowledge of the environmental repercussions, lack of political willingness to create soil policies that regulate soil use, uncertain land tenure, and the absence of legislative mechanisms are all reasons that hamper the development of sound soil governance in Chinandega. Hence, the societal *response* to the impacts (**Figure 2**) is insufficient to address the soil pollution sustainably. This vicious circle tends to maintain or deteriorate the current situation. Clearly, societal responses need to find other pathways that involve actors from different decision-making levels such as the local government and the landowners themselves. Most of the *drivers* and *pressures*, i.e., insecure agricultural food supply, income/labor issues, use of pesticides, land use change, and climate change need national legislation measures or political action from local governments in order to reverse the negative relations. The landowners however have a great potential to change their own fate by changing *pressures* such as land use and soil fertility management, which will positively influence *states* such as degraded soil, water quality, and contaminated crops and in the long run even *impacts* such as human health, low yields, limited opportunities for value creation, and biodiversity loss. The landowners may not currently possess the necessary knowledge to implement such a change in land use habits but change agents such as academia, and NGOs may promote the necessary knowledge transfer to catalyze such a change. NGOs can also promote an active citizenship that will put pressure on politicians and dissuade lack of political willingness.

Academia and NGOs operating in the region therefore plays a crucial role to stimulate the necessary changes of *drivers* and reduction of *pressures*. Institutional bodies such as universities (e.g., UNAN-Managua) in collaboration with their international scientific and educational partners (e.g., Mid Sweden University, University of Brasilia, Monaco's International Atomic Energy Agency, Technical University of Lisbon, Danish Aarhus University, Norwegian Institute for Water Research, etc.) have promoted scientific investigations on historical and current sources of contamination affecting soil, waters, crops, and human health. Although such research projects have increased the awareness within the scientific community, to date, this knowledge has not efficiently reached the local communities, nor has it brought forth responses by means of remediation projects.

Locally active NGOs (such as Proleña and Chinantlan) together with academia are therefore important drivers of change with great potential to influence public policy-making in terms of creating awareness of soil pollution problems and potential solutions. The low economic capacities and low priority given to soil pollution by local governments together with the predominantly private tenure of the land places a major responsibility for the remediation on the individual landowners [17, 65, 66]. NGOs and academia have a more direct impact by stimulating landowners to adopt multifunctional land-use strategies that address many of the regions sustainability problems simultaneously. Productive systems can be designed in a way that, in addition to remediating the soil, also provide a source of income or address other scopes of the common agenda and deliver perceivable, direct economic incentives for the landowners [17, 18]. Multifunctional land-use production systems (of food or biomass for energy) with capacity for phytoremediation are low-cost solutions compared to conventional physicochemical soil treatments. Such low-cost systems could potentially produce high outputs in terms of socio-ecological and economic benefits (e.g., more resilient agricultural systems, provision of societal goods and services, soil and water quality enhancement, biodiversity conservation, and reduction of poverty). In the case of Chinandega, a marginalized region with high dependence on agricultural production, these motivations are significant when it comes to the screening of alternatives to solve the soil contamination issue of the region and the consequences arising from it.

5. Prospects for sustainable remediation of polluted soil in developing countries

Sustainable remediation of polluted soils in developing countries must meet and surmount many challenges. Important challenges identified in this chapter relates to technology transitions and soil governance. Technologies for soil remediation in developing countries need to meet a different set of criteria than in industrialized countries and should be designed to meet the immediate socio-economic, cultural, and environment contexts in which they are introduced. Sustainable technology transitions must be aligned with the development and application of suitable legislation, policies, and standards. Improvements or development of new soil legislation and policies need to be locally adapted, match the latest scientific progress, and be flexible enough to allow innovative solutions. The DPSIR case study of the region Chinandega, Nicaragua demonstrates a number of drivers that lead to unsustainable production and consumption patterns that in turn adds pressure to both agricultural and natural systems in the region. Past pressures (e.g., excessive use of persistent pesticides) and external pressures due to climate change complicate the situation and aggravate the effects of misuse of natural resources and land. The result is toxic and degraded land (state) that is detrimental to the ecosystems, people's health and to opportunities for value-creation from agriculture production. The responses are currently insufficient to promote sustainable land use, but the DPSIR analysis suggests some ways forward. To address the pollution problem, academia and NGOs have a crucial role as change agents to support policy-makers and farmers with decision support and promote multifunctional strategies that can remediate polluted soil but also provide a source of income or/and address other scopes of the common agenda. An important learning outcome of this DPSIR analysis, which is applicable to other regions in developing countries, is that soil governance at all decision-making levels should be aligned to promote cooperation between academia, NGOs and policy-makers that jointly can stimulate a gradual change toward sustainability and reduction of the soil pool of pollutants.

Acknowledgements

We thank Dr. Martha Lacayo, Marta Jarquín Pascua, Maybis López Hernández, and the other members of the team at the Biotechnology Laboratory of UNAN-Managua, for their great support with the field research in Chinandega. We also thank Ajax Fonseca and Francisco Javier Espinoza (project leader and General Coordinator, respectively) from the Chinantlan Cooperative Association for their assistance during the study visits at different farms.

Author details

Henrik Haller*, Ginnette Flores-Carmenate and Anders Jonsson
Department of Ecotechnology and Sustainable Building Engineering, Östersund, Sweden

*Address all correspondence to: henrik.haller@miun.se

References

[1] Wesseling C, Aragón A, Castillo L, Corriols M, Chaverri F, Cruz EDL, et al. Hazardous pesticides in Central America. International Journal of Occupational and Environmental Health. 2001;7(4):287-294

[2] Molina-Barahona L, Vega-Loyo L, Guerrero M, Ramirez S, Romero I, Vega-Jarquín C, et al. Ecotoxicological evaluation of diesel-contaminated soil before and after a bioremediation process. Environmental Toxicology. 2005;**20**(1):100-109

[3] Ortiz-Hernández ML, Rodríguez A, Sánchez-Salinas E, Castrejón-Godínez ML. Bioremediation of Soils Contaminated with Pesticides: Experiences in Mexico. I: Bioremediation in Latin America. Cham: Springer; 2014. pp. 69-99

[4] Rodríguez-Eugenio N, McLaughlin M, Pennock D. Soil Pollution: A Hidden Reality. Rome: FAO; 2018

[5] Yu L, Zhu J, Huang Q, Su D, Jiang R, Li H. Application of a rotation system to oilseed rape and rice fields in Cd-contaminated agricultural land to ensure food safety. Ecotoxicology and Environmental Safety. 2014;**108**:287

[6] Nellemann C, Corcoran E. Dead Planet, Living Planet: Biodiversity and Ecosystem Restoration for Sustainable Development. GRID-Arendal: United Nations Environment Programme (UNEP); 2010

[7] Bridges EM. World map of the status of humaninduced soil degradation, oldeman, L. R., Hakkeling, R. T. A. and Sombroek, W. G. UNEP/ISRIC, Nairobi, Kenya, 1990. Isbn 90 6672 042 5, US$25.00 (paperback), 3 maps and explanatory note + 27 pp. Land Degradation & Development. 1992;**3**(1):68-69

[8] FAO. Be the Solution to Soil Pollution - Proceedings of the Global Symposium on Soil Pollution Rome. Italy: FAO; 2018

[9] Sverdrup HU, Ragnarsdottir KV, Koca D. An assessment of metal supply sustainability as an input to policy: Security of supply extraction rates, stocks-in-use, recycling, and risk of scarcity. Journal of Cleaner Production. 2017;**140**:359-372

[10] van der Voet E, Salminen R, Eckelman M, Norgate T, Mudd G, Hisschier R, et al. Environmental Challenges of Anthropogenic Metals Flows and Cycles, A Report of the Working Group on the Global Metal Flows to the International Resource Panel. Nairobi: United Nations Environment Programme; 2013

[11] McLaughlin M. Red. Drivers of soil pollution in agricultural fields. In: Proceedings of the Global Symposium on Soil Pollution; 2-4 May 2018. Rome: Italy Food and Agriculture Organisation (FAO); 2018

[12] Ongley ED, Booty WG. Pollution remediation planning in developing countries: Conventional modelling versus knowledge-based prediction. Water International. 1999;**24**(1):31-38

[13] UNEP. Towards a Pollution-Free Planet. Nairobi, Kenya: UNEP; 2017

[14] Singh B, Gupta S, Azaizeh H, Shilev S, Sudre D, Song W, et al. Safety of food crops on land contaminated with trace elements. Journal of the Science of Food and Agriculture. 2011;**91**:1349-1366

[15] Duruibe JO, Ogwuegbu M, Egwurugwu J. Heavy metal pollution and human biotoxic effects. International Journal of Physical Sciences. 2007;**2**(5):112-118

[16] Qu C-S, Ma Z-W, Yang J, Liu Y, Bi J, Huang L. Human exposure pathways of heavy metals in a lead-zinc mining area, Jiangsu Province, China. PLoS One. 2012;**7**(11):e46793

[17] Haller H, Jonsson A, Fröling M. Application of ecological engineering within the framework for strategic sustainable development for design of appropriate soil bioremediation technologies in marginalized regions. Journal of Cleaner Production. 2018;**172**:2415-2424

[18] Jonsson A, Haller H. Sustainability aspects of in-situ bioremediation of polluted soil in developing countries and remote regions. In: I: Environmental Risk Assessment of Soil Contamination, Environmental Risk Assessment of Soil Contamination, Maria C. Hernandez-Soriano. Rijeka: IntechOpen. 2014. DOI: 10.5772/57315

[19] Haller H. Soil Remediation and Sustainable Development - Creating Appropriate Solutions for Marginalized Regions. Doctoral Dissertation. Östersund: Mid Sweden University; 2017

[20] Kovalick WW Jr, Montgomery RH. Developing a Program for Contaminated Site Management in low and Middle Income Countries. Washington DC: International Bank for Reconstruction and Development/The world Bank; 2014

[21] Mench M, Lepp N, Bert V, Schwitzguébel J-P, Gawronski SW, Schröder P, et al. Successes and limitations of phytotechnologies at field scale: Outcomes, assessment and outlook from COST action 859. Journal of Soils and Sediments. 2010;**10**(6):1039-1070

[22] Tang Y-T, Deng T-H-B, Wu Q-H, Wang S-Z, Qiu R-L, Wei Z-B, et al. Designing cropping Systems for Metal-Contaminated Sites: A review. Pedosphere. 2012;**22**(4):470-488

[23] Boopathy R. Factors limiting bioremediation technologies. Bioresource Technology. 2000;**74**(1):63-67

[24] Gutberlet J. Rural development and social exclusion: A case study of sustainability and distributive issues in Brazil. Australian Geographer. 1999;**30**(2):221-237

[25] Macfarlane S, Racelis M, Muli-Muslime F. Public health in developing countries. The Lancet. 2000;**356**(9232):841-846

[26] Elands BH, Wiersum KF. Forestry and rural development in Europe: An exploration of socio-political discourses. Forest Policy and Economics. 2001;**3**(1):5-16

[27] Orcao AIE, Cornago CD. Accessibility to basic services in one of the most sparsely populated areas in Europe: The province of Teruel (Spain). Area. 2007;**39**(3):295-309

[28] Saith R. Social Exclusion: The Concept and Application to Developing Countries. Oxford: Queen Elizabeth House; 2001

[29] Lee E, Vivarelli M. The social impact of globalization in the developing countries. International Labour Review. 2006;**145**:167

[30] Romijn H, Raven R, de Visser I. Biomass energy experiments in rural India: Insights from learning-based development approaches and lessons for strategic niche management. Environmental Science and Policy. 2010;**13**(4):326-338

[31] Ramos-Mejía M, Franco-Garcia M-L, Jauregui-Becker JM. Sustainability transitions in the developing world: Challenges of socio-technical transformations unfolding in contexts of poverty. Environmental Science and Policy. 2018;**84**:217-223

[32] Ostrom E, Janssen MA, Anderies JM. Going beyond panaceas. (SPECIAL FEATURE: INTRODUCTORY PERSPECTIVE) (socio-ecological systems) (report). Proceedings of the National Academy of Sciences of the United States of America. 2007;**104**(39):15176

[33] Yáñez L, Ortiz D, Calderón J, Batres L, Carrizales L, Mejía J, et al. Overview of human health and chemical mixtures: Problems facing developing countries. Environmental Health Perspectives. 2002;**110**(Suppl 6): 901-909

[34] Mohee R, Mudhoo A. Bioremediation and Sustainability: Research and Applications. New Jersey: John Wiley & Sons; 2012

[35] Castree N, Kitchin R, Rogers A. A Dictionary of Human Geography. Oxford: Oxford University Press; 2013

[36] Evans DD. Appropriate technology and its role in development. Appropriate technology for development: a discussion and case histories; 1984

[37] Hazeltine B, Bull C. Appropriate Technology: Tools, Choices, and Implications. Cambridge, Massachusetts: Academic Press, Inc.; 1998

[38] Schumacher EF. Small Is Beautiful: A Study of Economics as if People Mattered. Ney York: Random House; 2011

[39] Murphy HM, McBean EA, Farahbakhsh K. Appropriate technology–a comprehensive approach for water and sanitation in the developing world. Technology in Society. 2009;**31**(2):158-167

[40] Ranis G. Appropriate Technology and the Development Process. Cambridge, USA: Ballinger Publishing Company; 1980. pp. 99-120

[41] Razikordmahaleh L. Red. Policy research on soil contamination to achieve food safety. In: Proceedings of the Global Symposium on Soil Pollution; 2-4 May 2018. Rome: Italy Food and Agriculture Organisation (FAO); 2018

[42] FAO. Proceedings of the Global Symposium on Soil Pollution 2018. Rome, Italy: Food and Agriculture Organization of the United Nations; 2018

[43] FAO, ITPS. Status of the world's Soil Resources: Main Report. Rome, Italy: FAO; 2015

[44] Castelo-Grande T, Augusto PA, Fiúza A, Barbosa D. Strengths and weaknesses of European soil legislations: The case study of Portugal. Environmental Science and Policy. 2018;**79**:66-93

[45] Ramón Fernández F, Lull C. Legal approach to measures to prevent soil contamination and increase food safety for the consumer. I: (FAO) FaAO, red. In: Proceedings of the Global Symposium on Soil Pollution; 2-4 May 2018. Rome: Italy Food and Agriculture Organisation (FAO); 2018

[46] Wassenaar T, Feder F, Doelsch E. Assessing agricultural soil pollution risks from organic waste recycling: Informing regional participatory waste management. In: Proceedings of the Global Symposium on Soil Pollution; 2-4 May 2018. Rome: Italy Food and Agriculture Organisation (FAO); 2018

[47] Luppi B, Parisi F, Rajagopalan S. The rise and fall of the polluter-pays principle in developing countries. International Review of Law and Economics. 2012;**32**(1):135-144

[48] Li T, Liu Y, Lin S, Liu Y, Xie Y. Soil pollution Management in China: A brief introduction. Sustainability. 2019;**11**:556

[49] Anelli S, Gregori A, Iavazzo P, Leonardi L, Nastasio P, Prandelli A, et al. Transfer of contaminants from agricultural contaminated soils to crop plants: A field study at Brescia-Caffaro SIN (Italy). I: (FAO) FaAO, red. In: Proceedings of the Global Symposium on Soil Pollution; 2-4 May 2018. Rome: Italy Food and Agriculture Organisation (FAO); 2018

[50] Miroshnychenko M, Hladkikh Y, Solovey V, Lykova O. Setting the thresholds for heavy metals based on their background & soil resilience. I: (FAO) FaAO, red. In: Proceedings of the Global Symposium on Soil Pollution; 2-4 May 2018. Rome: Italy Food and Agriculture Organisation (FAO); 2018

[51] Clostre F, Letourmy P, Lesueur-Jannoyer M. Soil thresholds and a decision tool to manage food safety of crops grown in chlordecone polluted soil in the French West Indies. Environmental Pollution. 2017;**223**:357-366

[52] Rothstein H, Irving P, Walden T, Yearsley R. The risks of risk-based regulation: Insights from the environmental policy domain. Environment International. 2006;**32**(8):1056-1065

[53] Plant JA, Bone J, Ragnarsdottir KV, Voulvoulis N. Pollutants, human health and the environment – A risk-based approach. Applied Geochemistry. 2011;**26S**:S238-SS40

[54] Sareen SA. Scheme and Training Manual on Good Agricultural Practices. Rome: FAO; 2016

[55] Huysegoms L, Cappuyns V. Critical review of decision support tools for sustainability assessment of site remediation options. Journal of Environmental Management. 2017;**196**:278-296

[56] Bell S. DPSIR= a problem structuring method? An exploration from the "imagine" approach. European Journal of Operational Research. 2012;**222**(2):350-360

[57] Carr ER, Wingard PM, Yorty SC, Thompson MC, Jensen NK, Roberson J. Applying DPSIR to sustainable development. International Journal of Sustainable Development and World Ecology. 2007;**14**(6):543-555

[58] Kristensen P. The DPSIR Framework. Denmark: National Environmental Research Institute; 2004. p. 10

[59] Ness B, Anderberg S, Olsson L. Structuring problems in sustainability science: The multi-level DPSIR framework. Geoforum. 2010;**41**(3):479-488

[60] Tscherning K, Helming K, Krippner B, Sieber S, Paloma SG. Does research applying the DPSIR framework support decision making? Land Use Policy. 2012;**29**(1):102-110

[61] Gari SR, Newton A, Icely JD. A review of the application and evolution of the DPSIR framework with an emphasis on coastal social-ecological systems. Ocean and Coastal Management. 2015;**103**:63-77

[62] Hisschemöller M, Tol RS, Vellinga P. The relevance of participatory approaches in integrated environmental assessment. Integrated Assessment. 2001;**2**(2):57-72

[63] Ravetz J. Integrated assessment for sustainability appraisal in cities and regions. Environmental Impact Assessment Review. 2000;**20**(1):31-64

[64] Tol RS, Vellinga P. The European forum on integrated environmental assessment. Environmental Modeling and Assessment. 1998;**3**(3):181-191

[65] Carvalho F, Montenegro-Guillén S, Villeneuve J, Cattini C, Tolosa I, Bartocci J, et al. Toxaphene residues from cotton fields in soils and in the coastal environment of Nicaragua. Chemosphere. 2003;**53**(6):627-636

[66] Corriols M. Pesticide poisoning in Nicaragua-five decades of evidence. Pesticides. 2010;**89**:3-6

[67] Moncrieff JE, Bentley LR, Palma HC. Investigating pesticide transport in the León-Chinandega aquifer, Nicaragua. Hydrogeology Journal. 2008;**16**(1):183-197

[68] Thornton RL, Hatt LE, Field EM, Islam M, Solís Diaz F, González MA. Social security health insurance for the informal sector in Nicaragua: A randomized evaluation. Health Economics. 2010;**19**(S1):181-206

[69] Gourdji S, Läderach P, Valle AM, Martinez CZ, Lobell DB. Historical climate trends, deforestation, and maize and bean yields in Nicaragua. Agricultural and Forest Meteorology. 2015;**200**:270-281

[70] Omann I, Stocker A, Jäger J. Climate change as a threat to biodiversity: An application of the DPSIR approach. Ecological Economics. 2009;**69**(1):24-31

Chapter 6

Studies, Efforts and Investigations on Various Aspects of Solid Waste Management with Emphasis on Developing Countries

Sunil Jayant Kulkarni

Abstract

Solid waste can be broadly classified as putrescible and non-putrescible based on its biodegradability. Municipal solid waste contains food waste, papers, plastic, paints, heavy metals and rubber. Industrial solid waste may contain waste adsorbent, waste catalyst sludge, solid residue of by-product, residue of reactions and hazardous materials also. Dewatering, centrifugal filtration, drying and incineration are usual steps used for solid waste treatment in industries. Biodegradable solid waste, being rich in organic content, can be used to synthesize various useful organic compounds. Vermicomposting is an effective method for converting organic waste into nutrient-rich fertilizer. Food and vegetable waste can be processed to obtain useful products. Inorganic domestic waste and electronic waste may contain valuable heavy metals like gold and platinum. E-waste and industrial waste containing hazardous waste need to be classified and treated carefully. Non-biodegradable waste like plastic and rubber can be reused or recycled. Non-government organizations in developing countries are playing key role in creating awareness among people about solid waste. Recycling in industries is promoted by government through various schemes and initiatives. This chapter briefly explains initiatives and investigations aimed at increasing adoptability and efficiency of various solid minimizations, reuse, recycle methods and technologies used for synthesis of value-added products.

Keywords: recycle, decomposition, fermentation, synthesis, yield, recovery

1. Introduction

Solid waste can be broadly classified as putrescible and non-putrescible, based on its biodegradability. Putrescible waste contains organic matter. This waste is suitable for digestion and land disposal. Non-putrescible waste is generally non-biodegradable waste which cannot be digested. Municipal solid waste contains food waste, papers, plastic, paints, heavy metals and rubber. Municipal waste needs to be classified based on biodegradability for further treatment. Local civic bodies are now putting stringent norms for classification of solid waste. In India green and blue containers are provided to households to separate this waste and source. Industrial solid waste may contain, waste adsorbent, waste catalyst sludge, solid residue of by-product, residue of reactions, etc. This solid waste may contain hazardous material also. Dewatering, centrifugal filtration, drying and incineration are usual steps used for solid waste treatment in industries. Bio-degradable solid waste, rich in organic content can be used to synthesize various useful organic compounds. Non-biodegradable waste like plastic, rubber can be reused or recycled. Reduce, reuse and recycle are nowadays trending concepts in solid waste management. Non-government organizations (NGOs) in developing countries are playing key role in developing awareness among people about proper segregation and collection of solid waste. Recycling industry is promoted by government through various schemes and initiatives. This chapter briefly explains initiatives and investigations aimed at various solid minimizations, reuse and recycle methods and methods used for synthesis of value-added products from solid wastes. Initiatives taken by governments; non-government organizations are briefed in the chapter. Also, investigations carried out by scientific community to treat and recycle solid waste are reviewed. The chapter contains efforts taken for solid waste recycle and reuse in Asian countries, though it contains some significant efforts in other developing countries also. This review is based on available literature, research papers and available reports on solid waste management.

2. Methodology

Solid waste contains bio-degradable and non-bio-degradable material. Non-bio-degradable material cannot be digested and hence reuse or recycle of this type of waste is becoming important area of investigation. Countries like China, Taiwan and Malaysia are taking initiatives to reduce plastic waste by reuse and recycle principle. First three sections (Sections 3–5) of the chapter are devoted to plastic and non-bio-degradable waste. In remaining sections, reuse, recycle, recovery and energy generation methods for biodegradable waste are explained with the help of available literature and research papers. Domestic and municipal solid waste treatment needs to be more familiar with people. For this, efforts are being taken by government authorities by adopting regulations and stricter norms. These regulations along with awareness created by social groups and organizations can improve waste management scenario in developing countries. Another aspect of solid waste treatment discussed in this chapter is investigations carried out by researchers to optimize the waste reuse and recycle technologies. This aspect is briefed with the help of research papers published by investigators from these developing countries.

3. Plastic bags

Plastic bags are used for containing and transporting goods. Also, they are used for vegetables, groceries and other domestic items as a container. Plastic, which sometimes is non-replaceable, is very important material if used sensibly. The plastic bags are very thin and flexible. The disposal of these plastic bags is creating huge problems in developing countries. If these bags are recycled, the disposal problem would not arise. But lack of awareness and willpower has played a great roll in plastic ban. Nowadays the governments have banned the use of plastic bags above certain thickness. Even many other civic bodies are banning plastic use. Studies show that increase in reuse of plastic can reduce the eco-impact of plastic to a great extent [1]. In developing countries, blockage of drainage due to plastic causes calamities such as flood. Also, it can be a reason for mosquito breeding. Lack of sophistication of the recycle and waste treatment facility develops concern about manufacture and use of plastic [2]. Many developing countries in

Africa have adopted use of glass container instead of plastic. They are promoting use of cloth bags instead of plastic bags [3, 4].

4. Waste plastic

Waste plastic and rubber can be used in road construction [5]. Semi-dense bitumen concrete can be prepared and used for road construction. Waste plastic material such as high-density polyethylene (HDPE-2), low-density polyethylene (LDPE-4), poly propylene (PP-5) and polystyrene (PS-6) can be used for obtaining different products [6]. Slurry formation, liquefaction, recovery and condensation are the steps in the process. Use of superplasticizer can enhance the properties of waste plastic in road construction [7]. Biomedical plastic waste finds application in road construction. Compared to normal the bituminous mix, bio-medical plastic waste coated mix had better properties [8]. Pyrolysis oil can be derived from the waste plastic and can be used to derive diesel. Studies indicate that this diesel is suitable for use in engine [9]. Use of plastic waste in the flexible pavements increases strength and durability [10, 11]. Bitumen requirement can be reduced by 8–12% by using plastic waste for pavement material [12]. Thermal cracking of waste plastic can convert them into usable oil form [13]. Also, plastic bottles can be used for the construction of house. It is observed that these houses are bioclimatic. It means that when it is cold outside is warm inside and vice versa [14].

5. E-waste

Discarded, obsolete, end of life electrical and electronics equipment forms Electronic waste (E-waste). Heavy metals such as lead, cadmium, chromium, mercury, barium is present in E-waste [15]. The E-waste recycling needs quantitative measures for recycling and reuse of E-waste [16]. Illegally imported E-waste from developed countries is additional E-waste problem faced by India like countries [17]. There is need for increasing awareness about health effects of E-waste and importance of recycling. Inventorization and unhealthy conditions of informal recycling, inadequate legislation, poor awareness and reluctance on part of the corporate to address solid waste issues are drawbacks of waste minimization programs in India [18]. Waste materials from discarded computers, televisions, stereos, copiers, fax machines, electric lamps, cell phones, audio equipment and batteries can be hazardous to health. For example, lead can leach out from the E-waste materials, and enter into human bodies through oral route [19]. According to Kumar and Shah, the crude recycling activities cause irreversible health and environmental hazards [20]. So, there is need of refinement of the process adopted for recycle. According to Kumar and Karishma, India is fifth largest producer of E-waste in the world. In India only recycling of E-waste is 10% of recycle business [21]. About 65% of E-waste is generated in urban Area in India [21]. About 21% of this E-waste is plastic. E-waste is fastest growing waste stream in the world [22, 23]. Around seven lakh tons of E-waste were produced in India in 2016 [24]. Individual and government contributions can help to tackle this E-waste problem [25]. It is important to bridge the gap between the formal and informal divide in E-waste management in India [26]. E-waste recycling provides jobs to thousands of people in India. There needs to be coordination between formal and non-formal sectors for proper treatment and recycling of E-waste. There is need for the collection, segregation and primary dismantling of non-hazardous fractions of E-waste. Compatible and efficient technology for E-waste was a matter of concern for India and many developing countries. According to Vats and Singh, informal recyclers are treating 95% of the E-waste generated with hazardous practices [27].

6. Food waste utilization for product synthesis

Food waste can be used for synthesis of various useful chemicals. Source separated food waste can be used for synthesis of ethanol with thermophilic enzymes [28]. Food waste biomass can be used in treating wastewater. Anaerobic digestion of this waste upon acidogenesis produces volatile fatty acids [29]. Ethanol cultivated biomass can be used effectively for the effluent of the food waste digestion. Food waste can be processed in long-term operation of a laboratory anaerobic reactor in mesophilic conditions for anaerobic fermentation to produce biogas and useful products [30]. Shukla et al. have explored the possibility of biohydrogen production from food waste [31]. Degradation of food waste and energy recovery through biogas production are twin benefits of the anaerobic digestion [32]. Factors such as organic loading rate, temperature, time, pH, carbon to nitrogen ratio play vital role in the process. With increase in methanogenic bacteria, the methane percent in biogas increases significantly [33]. An investigation by Akpan indicated that producing ethanol from food waste is more economical than producing it from other waste organic sources like old newspapers [34]. For synthesis of biohydrogen from waste, methods such as the methods like electrolysis of water, steam reforming of hydrocarbons and auto-thermal processes can be used [35]. According to Kapdan and Kargi, use of photosynthetic algae is one of the important methods for hydrogen synthesis from waste [36]. Investigations are reported on synthesis of bioplastic from food waste. Ingredients from food waste such as starch, cellulose, fatty acids, sugars and proteins can be used for bioplastic synthesis [37]. Many investigations are reported on hydrolysis of food waste and subsequent ethanol formation [38, 39]. Various investigations are reported on synthesis of lactic acid, vinegar and citric acid from waste materials including food waste [40–43].

7. Aerobic treatment methods for food waste

Anaerobic methods reduce the sludge volume significantly and produce biogas fuel. Major disadvantage of this method is that it causes nuisance to nearby population [44, 45]. Aerobic thermophiling composting reduces odor problem [46]. pH, temperature, moisture content, organic carbon, volatile solids are vital factors during aerobic composting [47]. Also, C/N ratio and volume reduction are performance indicators of the process [48]. Obtaining optimal performance system is very vital in increasing acceptability of the waste treatment method [49]. Waste management strategy includes many steps such as disposal, treatment, reduction, recycling, segregation and modification [50].

8. Vermicomposting for domestic solid waste

Vermicomposting has advantages over aerobic and anaerobic digestion methods as it overcomes few drawbacks like odor, space and cost of these two methods. Vermicomposting is a method used to convert organic waste into fertilizers with the help of worms. Factors affecting the process are parameters like the growth rate (pH), number of worms, number of cocoons and worm biomass [51]. Bedding material has also influence on the process. Newspaper bedding was effective in the investigation carried out by Manaf et al. [51]. Studies have shown that vermicomposting improves the soil structure, enhancing soil fertility, moisture holding capacity and in turn increase the crop yield [52, 53]. Vermicomposting derived liquid can be used for agriculture [54]. This liquid has very high nutrient value. Studies confirm that home composting has potential to reduce the greenhouse gas emission [55]. Investigation carried out by Kulkarni and Sose indicated that pH values between 6.4 and 7.6 are favorable for vermicomposting. 30–50% moisture is required for vermicomposting [56]. Optimum temperature lies between 25 and 30°C.

9. Paper waste

Paper waste can be used for applications like biofuel synthesis and ceiling boards, bioelectricity production, and fuel gas generation. Also, it can be used in mixed concrete. Papers are normally recycled. In order to prepare good quality paper only limited number of recycles can be done. So finally, it results into huge amount of waste, this waste sludge can be used in the concrete up to 30% concentration, as investigation revealed that up to 30% addition the concrete quality increases and it decreases after that [57]. Also, waste paper sludge can be used for biofuel synthesis. The sludge can be converted into simple fermentable sugar by microbial process [58]. The waste sludge can be mixed in 1:1 proportion with calcium carbonate additive to form good quality ceiling boards [59]. Detachment of ink from the-waste papers increases their drainability [60]. According to Allahvakil et al. [60], it is possible to modify the chemical or physical bonds with enzymes such as pectinase, cellulase and hemicellulose. This helps in detachment of ink from the paper. The waste papers can also be used as raw material for bioelectricity generation. Microbial fuel cell with Clostridium species can be used for the purpose [61]. According to research carried out by Mathuria and Sharma [61], a microwave plasma reactor can be used for conversion of waste papers to fuel gas. Waste paper sludge ash can be used for stabilization of clay soil. An investigation by Khalid et al. [62] indicated that the waste sludge ash up to 10% can exhibit excellent binding properties in the clay. According to Arshad and Pawade [63], the addition of waste paper also reduces the quantity of clay required.

10. Gold recovery from solid waste

Electronic and mobile component contain valuable materials like gold and platinum. Ammonium thiosulfate can be used for leaching gold from mobile circuit boards [64]. According to Chehade et al. [65], the printed circuit board contains about 0.15% of gold. Aqua regia can be used as a leaching agent for recovery of gold [66]. This process can be automized to provide solution to gold recovery [67]. Fibrous ion exchange resins can improve gold and platinum recovery. Catalyst industry waste contains gold, platinum and valuable metals [68]. About 3 vol% NaClO, 5 kmol/m^3 HCl and 1 vol% H_2O_2 can be used for leaching platinum compounds [69]. In case of hydrochloric acid (HCl), the recovery is 99%. Platinum and gold removal from the industrial waste is necessity from ecological and environmental point of view [70].

11. Biogas production

Factors such as pH, organic loading, moisture content plays significant role in biogas production. Various types of biomass like fruit waste, domestic waste and crop residues can be used for biogas production. Pineapple waste biomass 48%

concentration in biogas was obtained in less than 50 days [71]. Cow dung is also very good source of biomass. Paper waste exhibits highest methane concentration in biogas, about 73% than other solid wastes such as cow dung, saw dust, rice husk and millet waste. However, hydrogen sulfide concentration is highest in this biogas [72]. A mixture of equal percentage of paper waste and biomass can be used for biogas production to increase quality of biogas. It is observed that the biogas production increases by 50% than paper waste alone. In case of orange peels, it is needed to pre-treat the peels as that content limonene, which is antimicrobial [73]. Many such investigations are reported on biogas synthesis from various type of solid waste [74–77]. Disposal of the final sludge from treatment plants needs to undergo drying and further incineration or dumping of dry biomass [78].

12. Bioconversion of waste feed stock

Putrescible solid waste like food and fruit waste, food grain waste, vegetable waste can be used for production of various products by employing bioconversion with suitable bacteria or microorganism [79]. Single cell protein can be obtained from orange peels and cucumber peel by using *Aspergillus niger* and *Saccharomyces cerevisiae* [79, 80]. These investigations suggested that glucose addition to the supplemented fruit hydrolysate medium. Solid state fermentation of orange peels with *Aspergillus niger* yields pectinase [81]. Content of ammonium sulfate, glucose and water in the culture medium affects the process [81]. Ethanol synthesis from fruit and other biodegradable waste is very common method of utilizing waste [82–87]. Number of other products such as citric acid, acetic acid, lactic acid, lactic acid, etc. can be obtained by using suitable microorganisms and operating conditions [84–87]. These conditions differ from product to product and waste type.

13. Hazardous waste

Hazardous waste poses serious problem to human being and environment. These hazardous wastes may contain biological waste, nuclear waste, heavy metals and flammable materials to considerable extent. Stricter laws and their implementation are required to save the environmental from the hazardous waste [88]. Proper classification and monitoring of hazardous waste can help to treat the waste efficiently [89]. Incineration and recycling are two most sustainable waste management practices [90, 91].

14. Conclusion

Bio-degradable solid waste, rich in organic content can be used to synthesize various useful organic compounds. Non-biodegradable waste like plastic, rubber can be reused or recycled. Reduce, reuse and recycle are nowadays trending concepts in solid waste management. Non-government organizations (NGOs) in developing countries are playing key role in developing awareness among people about proper segregation and collection of solid waste. Recycling industry is promoted by government through various schemes and initiatives. Local civic bodies are now putting stringent norms for classification of solid waste. In India green and blue containers are provided to households to separate this waste and source. Industrial solid waste may contain, waste adsorbent, waste catalyst sludge, solid residue of by-product, residue of reactions, etc. This solid waste may contain hazardous material also. Dewatering, centrifugal filtration, drying and incineration are usual steps used for solid waste treatment in industries. In developing countries, blockage of drainage due to plastic causes calamities such as flood. Also, it can be a reason for mosquito breeding. Lack of sophistication of the recycle and waste treatment facility develops concern about manufacture and use of plastic. Following observations were made based on study of literature on solid waste treatment.

- Many developing countries in Africa have adopted use of glass container instead of plastic.
- Compatible and efficient technology for E-waste was a matter of concern for India and many developing countries.
- Various investigations are reported on synthesis of lactic acid, vinegar and citric acid from waste materials including food waste.
- Waste management strategy includes many steps such as disposal, treatment, reduction, recycling, segregation and modification.
- Various types of biomass like fruit waste, domestic waste and crop residues can be used for biogas production.
- Studies have shown that vermicomposting improves the soil structure, enhancing soil fertility, moisture holding capacity and in turn increase the crop yield.
- Paper waste can be used for applications like biofuel synthesis and ceiling boards, bioelectricity production, and fuel gas generation. Also, it can be used in mixed concrete.
- Hazardous waste poses serious problem to human being and environment. These hazardous wastes may contain biological waste, nuclear waste, heavy metals and flammable materials to considerable extent. Stricter laws and their implementation are required to save the environmental from the hazardous waste.
- Platinum and gold removal from the industrial waste is necessity from ecological and environmental point of view.

Author details

Sunil Jayant Kulkarni
Chemical Engineering Department, Gharda Institute of Technology, Ratnagiri, Maharashtra, India

*Address all correspondence to: suniljayantkulkarni@gmail.com

References

[1] Muthu SSK, Li Y, Hu JY, Mok PY, Ding X. Eco-impact of plastic and paper shopping bags. Journal of Engineered Fibers and Fabrics. 2012;7(1):26-37

[2] Dana Gopal NM, Phebel P, Suresh Kumar EV, Vani BKK. Impact of plastic leading environmental pollution, national seminar on impact of toxic metals, minerals and solvents leading to environmental pollution-2014. Journal of Chemical and Pharmaceutical Sciences. 2014;(JCHPS Special Issue 3): 96-99

[3] Adane L, Muleta D. Survey on the usage of plastic bags, their disposal and adverse impacts on environment: A case study in Jimma City, Southwestern Ethiopia. Journal of Toxicology and Environmental Health Sciences. 2011;**3**(8):234-248

[4] Bashir NHH. Plastic problem in Africa. Japanese Journal of Veterinary Research. 2013;**61**(Supplement):S1-S11

[5] Rokade S. Use of waste plastic and waste rubber tyres in flexible highway pavements. In: International Conference on Future Environment and Energy Ipcbee. Vol. 28. Singapore: IACSIT Press; 2012. pp. 105-108

[6] Sarker M, Rashid MM, Molla M. Waste plastic conversion into chemical product like naphtha. Journal of Fundamentals of Renewable Energy and Applications. 2011;**1**:1-6

[7] Rai B, Rushad ST, Kr B, Duggal SK. Study of waste plasticmix concrete with plasticizer. International Scholarly Research Network. 2012;**2012**:1-5

[8] Bhageerathy KP, Alex AP, Manju VS, Raji AK. Use of biomedical plastic waste in bituminous road construction. International Journal of Engineering and Advanced Technology. 2014;**3**(6):89-92

[9] Sharma MC, Soni N. Production of alternative diesel fuel from waste oils and comparison with fresh diesel: A review. The International Journal of Engineering and Science. 2013;**3**(4):54-58

[10] Wayal AS, Wagle MD. Use of waste plastic and waste rubber in aggregate and bitumen for road materials. International Journal of Emerging Technology and Advanced Engineering. 2013;**3**(7):301-306

[11] Swami V, Jirge A, Patil K, Patil S, Patil S, Salokhe K. Use of waste plastic in construction of bituminous road. International Journal of Engineering Science and Technology. 2012;**4**(5):2351-2355

[12] Chavan AJ. Use of plastic waste in flexible pavements. International Journal of Application or Innovation in Engineering and Management. 2013;**2**(2):540-552

[13] Abatneh Y, Sahu O. Preliminary study on the conversion of different waste plastics into fuel oil. International Journal of Scientific & Technology Research. 2013;**2**(5):226-229

[14] Mohammad Salman Patel RA, Jadhwar NB, Khan U. Investigating the application of waste plastic bottle as a construction material: A review. Journal of the International Association of Advanced Technology and Science. 2015;**16**(16):1-16

[15] Shagun AK, Arora A. Proposed solution of E-waste management. International Journal of Future Computer and Communication. 2013;**2**(5):490493

[16] Sinha-Khetriwala D, Kraeuchib P, Schwaninger M. A comparison of electronic waste recycling in Switzerland and in India.

Environmental Impact Assessment Review. 2005;**25**:492-504

[17] Borthakur A, Singh P. Electronic waste in India: Problems and policies. International Journal of Environmental Sciences. 2012;**3**(1):353-362

[18] Joseph K. Electronic waste management in India–Issues and strategies. In: Proceedings Sardinia 2007, Eleventh International Waste Management and Landfill Symposium S. Margherita di Pula, Cagliari, Italy; 1-5 October 2007. 2007. pp. 1-9

[19] Ramachandra TV, Saira VK. Environment ally sound options for E-wastes management, Energy & Wetlands Research Group, Centre for Ecological Sciences, Indian Institute of Science Bangalore. 2004. p. 18. Available from: https://www.researchgate.net/publication/257137715_Environmentally_Sound_OptiOns_For_Ewastes_Management

[20] Kumar R, Shah DJ. Review: Current status of recycling of waste printed circuit boards in India. Journal of Environmental Protection. 2014;**5**:9-16

[21] Kumar R, Karishma. Current scenario of E-waste management in India: Issues and strategies. International Journal of Scientific and Research Publications. 2016;**6**(1):424-430

[22] Nair A, Hari N. Management of informal E-waste recycling with special reference to India. International Journal of Innovative Science, Engineering and Technology. 2015;**2**(3):45-52

[23] Jayapradha A. Scenario of E-waste in India and application of new recycling approaches for E-waste management. Journal of Chemical and Pharmaceutical Research. 2015;**7**(3):232-238

[24] Kumar S, Singh R, Singh D, Prasad R, Yadav T. Electronics-waste management. International Journal of Environmental Engineering and Management. 2013;**4**(4):389-396

[25] Begum KJA. Electronic waste (E-waste) management in India: A review. IOSR Journal of Humanities and Social Science (IOSR-JHSS). 2013;**10**(4):46-57

[26] Raghupathy L, Kruger C, Chaturvedi A, Arora R, Henzler MP. E-waste Recycling in India—Bridging the Gap Between the Informal and Formal Sector. 2015. pp. 1-10. Available from: http://www.iswa.org/uploads/tx_iswaknowledgebase/Krueger.pdf

[27] Vats MC, Singh SK. Status of E-waste in India—A review. International Journal of Innovative Research in Science, Engineering and Technology. 2014;**3**(10):16917-16931

[28] Matsakas L, Christakopoulos P. Ethanol production from enzymatically treated dried food waste using enzymes produced on-site. Sustainability. 2015;**7**:1446-1458

[29] Moukamnerd C, Kawahara H, Katakura Y. Feasibility study of ethanol production from food wastes by consolidated continuous solid-state fermentation. Journal of Sustainable Bioenergy Systems. 2013;**3**:143-148

[30] Fazeli G. Application of anaerobic digestion of municipal solid food wastes in treating wastewaters. International Journal of Human Capital in Urban Management. 2016;**1**(1):57-64

[31] Shukla B, Panjanathan R, Yadav A. Analysis of bio hydrogen production propensity of mixed consortium on food waste—A preliminary study. International Journal of Environmental Sciences. 2014;**5**(1):51-57

[32] Oliveira F, Doelle K. Anaerobic digestion of food waste to produce biogas: A comparison of bioreactors to increase methane content—A review. Journal of Food Processing & Technology. 2015;**6**(8):1-3

[33] Kader F, Baky AH, Khan MNH, Chowdhury HA. Production of biogas by anaerobic digestion of food waste and process simulation. American Journal of Mechanical Engineering. 2015;**3**(3):79-83

[34] Akpan UG, Alhakim AA, Ijah UJJ. Production of ethanol fuel from organic and food wastes. Leonardo Electronic Journal of Practices and Technologies. 2008;**13**:1-11

[35] Dlabaja T, Malatak J. Optimization of anaerobic fermentation of kitchen waste. Research in Agricultural Engineering. 2013;**59**(1):1-8

[36] Kapdan IK, Kargi F. Bio-hydrogen production from waste materials. Enzyme and Microbial Technology. 2006;**38**:569582

[37] Bubacz M, Goldsberry A. Bioplastics made from industrial food wastes. In: 2014 ASEE Southeast Section Conference. American Society for Engineering Education; 2014. pp. 1-7

[38] Chiranjeevi T, Uma A, Radhika K, Baby Rani G, Prakasham RS, Srinivasa Rao P, et al. Enzymatic hydrolysis of market vegetable waste and subsequent ethanol fermentation-kinetic evaluation. Journal of Biochemical Technology. 2014;**5**(4):775-781

[39] Duhan JS, Kumar A, Tanwar SK. Bioethanol production from starchy part of tuberous plant (potato) using saccharomyces cerevisiae MTCC-170. African Journal of Microbiology Research. 2003;**7**(46):5253-5260

[40] Kulkarni SJ. An insight into research and studies on biogas generation from waste. International Journal of Research and Review. 2016;**3**(5):78-81

[41] Kulkarni SJ. Production of citric acid: A review on research and studies. International Journal of Advanced Research Foundation. 2015;**2**(11):17-19

[42] Kulkarni SJ. Research and studies on vinegar production—A review. International Journal of Scientific Research in Science and Technology. 2015;**1**(5):146-148

[43] Kulkarni SJ, Shinde NL, Goswami AK. A review on ethanol production from agricultural waste raw material. International Journal on Scientific Research in Science, Engineering and Technology. 2015;**1**(4):231-233

[44] Agrahari RP, Tiwari GN. The production of biogas using kitchen waste. International Journal of Energy Science. 2013;**3**(6):408-415

[45] Kulkarni SJ. Food waste utilization: An insight into research and studies. International Journal of Ethics in Engineering and Management Education. 2016;**3**(8):1-4

[46] Asnani PU. Solid waste management. India Infrastructure Report. 2006;**1**:161-190

[47] Narkhede SD. Combined aerobic composting of municipal solid waste and sewage sludge. Global Journal of Environmental Research. 2010;**4**(2):109-112

[48] Wadkar DV, Modak PR, Chavan VS. Aerobic thermophilic composting of municipal solid waste. International Journal of Engineering Science and Technology. 2013;**5**(3):716-718

[49] Alleman JE, Mitchell C. Solid-phase thermophilic aerobic reactor (star) processing of fecal, food, and plant

residues. In: Annual and Monthly Reports Advanced Life Support—NASA Specialized Center of Research and Training (AlsNscort). Vol. 1. 2006. pp. 1-27

[50] Hamer G. Solid waste treatment and disposal: Effects on public health and environmental safety. Biotechnology Advances. 2003;**22**:71-79

[51] Manaf LA, Jusoh MLC, Yusoff MK, Ismail THT, Harun R, Juahir H. Influences of bedding material in vermicomposting process. International Journal of Biology. 2009;**1**(1):81-91

[52] Subbulakshmi G, Thiruneelakandan R. Vermicomposting is valiant in vandalizing the waste material. International Journal of Plant Animal and Environmental Sciences. 2011;**1**(3):134-141

[53] Kulkarni SJ. Vermicomposting—A boon for waste minimization and soil quality. International Journal of Research and Review. 2017;**4**(2):76-81

[54] Quaik S, Ibrahim MH. A review on potential of vermicomposting derived liquids in agricultural use. International Journal of Scientific and Research Publications. 2013;**3**(3):1-6

[55] Chan YC, Sinha RK, Wang W. Emission of greenhouse gases from home aerobic composting, anaerobic digestion and vermicomposting of household wastes in Brisbane (Australia). Waste Management and Research. 2010;**29**(5):540-548

[56] Sose MT, Kulkarni SJ. Studies and investigation on vermicomposting. International Journal of Research in Engineering and Technology. 2017;**06**(02):20-23

[57] Lenin Sundar M, Jeeva D, Vadivel M. Flexural behavior of concrete using waste paper sludge ash. International Journal of Earth Sciences and Engineering. 2016;**9**(3):497-500

[58] Prema D, Prabha ML, Gnanavel G. Production of biofuel using waste papers from *Pseudomonas aeruginosa*. International Journal of ChemTech Research. 2015;**8**(4):1803-1809

[59] Okeyinka OM, Idowu OJ. Assessment of the suitability of paper waste as an engineering material. Engineering, Technology & Applied Science Research. 2014;**4**(6):724-727

[60] Allahvakil H, Nikravesh B, Khatibzade M, Vajar H, Abbasi A, Najmi P. Enzymatic deinking on mixed office waste (MOW) papers. International Journal of Advances in Chemical Engineering and Biological Sciences. 2016;**3**(1):1-2

[61] Mathuriya AS, Sharma VN. Bioelectricity production from paper industry waste using a microbial fuel cell by Clostridium species. Journal of Biochemical Technology. 2009;**1**(2):49-52

[62] Khalid N, Mukri M, Kamarudin F, Arshad MF. Clay soil stabilized using waste paper sludge ash (WPSA) mixtures. EJGE. 2002;**17**:1215-1225

[63] Arshad MS, Pawade PY. Reuse of natural waste material for making light weight bricks. International Journal of Scientific & Technology Research. 2014;**3**(6):49-53

[64] Tripathi A, Manoj K, Sau DC, Agrawal A, Chakravarety S, Mankhand TR. Leaching of gold from the waste mobile phone printed circuit boards (Pcbs) with ammonium thiosulphate. International Journal of Metallurgical Engineering. 2012;**1**(2):17-21

[65] Chehade Y, Siddique A, Alayan H, Sadasivam N, Nusri S,

Ibrahim T. Recovery of gold, silver, palladium, and copper from waste printed circuit boards. In: International Conference on Chemical, Civil and Environment Engineering (Iccee'2012), March 24-25, 2012 Dubai. pp. 226-234

[66] Silvana D, Stevan D, Miric M. Recycling of precious metals from E-scrap. Iranian Journal of Chemistry and Chemical Engineering. 2013;**32**(4):17-23

[67] Hongal RN, Sunagad RG, Gombi SA, Patil R, Bhat K. A technical method of extraction of gold from E-waste: A multi-sensor based method using microcontroller. International Journal of Research in Engineering and Technology. 2014;**3**(7, sp. issue):94-97

[68] Ion exchange technology for the efficient recovery of precious metals from waste and low-grade streams. The Journal of the Southern African Institute of Mining and Metallurgy. 2014;**114**:173-182

[69] Harjanto S, Cao Y, Shibayama A, Naitoh I, Nanami T, Kasahara K, et al. Leaching of Pt, Pd and Rh from automotive catalyst residue in various chloride based solutions. Materials Transactions. 2006;**47**(1):129-135

[70] Kulkarni SJ. Removal and recovery of platinum: An insight into studies and research. International Journal of Research and Reviews. 2016;**3**(5):74-77

[71] ChulalaksananukulS,SinbuathongN, Chulalaksananukul W. Bioconversion of pineapple solid waste under anaerobic condition through biogas production. KKU Research Journal. 2012;**17**(5):734-742

[72] Bagudo BU, Garba B, Dangoggo SM, Hassan LG. The qualitative evaluation of biogas samples generated from selected organic wastes. Archives of Applied Science Research. 2011;**3**(5):549-555

[73] Ofoefule AU, Nwankwo JI, Ibeto CN. Biogas production from paper waste and its blend with cow dung. Advances in Applied Science Research. 2010;**1**(2):1-8

[74] Meggyes A, Nagy V. Biogas and energy production by utilization of different agricultural wastes. Acta Polytechnica Hungarica. 2012;**9**(6):6580

[75] Momoh OLY, Nwaogazie LI. Effect of waste paper on biogas production from co-digestion of cow dung and water hyacinth in batch reactors. Journal of Applied Sciences and Environmental Management. 2008;**12**(4):95-98

[76] Ray NHS, Mohanty MK, Mohanty RC. Anaerobic digestion of kitchen wastes: Biogas production and pre-treatment of wastes—A review. International Journal of Scientific and Research Publications. 2013;**3**(11):1-6

[77] Kulkarni SJ, Goswami AK. Characterization, treatment and disposal of sludge: A review. International Journal for Research in Applied Science and Engineering Technology. 2014;**2**(2):516-517

[78] Nandan A, Yadav B, Baksi S, Bose D. Recent scenario of solid waste management in India. World Scientific News. 2017;**66**:56-74

[79] Azam S, Khan Z, Hmad BA, Khan I, Ali J. Production of single cell protein from orange peels using *Aspergillus niger* and *Saccharomyces cerevisiae*. Global Journal of Biotechnology and Biochemistry. 2014;**9**(1):14-18

[80] Mondal AK, Sengupta S, Bhowal J, Bhattacharya DK. Utilization of fruit wastes in producing single cell protein. International Journal of Science, Environment and Technology. 2012, 2012;**1**(5):430-438

[81] Hachemi N, Nouani A, Benchabane A. Bioconversion of oranges wastes for pectinase production

using *Spergillus niger* under solid state fermentation. International Journal of Biological, Biomolecular, Agricultural, Food and Biotechnological Engineering. 2015;**9**(9):983-988

[82] Bekmuradov V. Bioconversion process of source separated organic waste for ethanol production [dissertation]. Ryerson University in Partial Fulfilment of the Requirements for the Degree of Doctor; 2015

[83] Raikar RV. Enhanced production of ethanol from grape waste. International Journal of Environmental Sciences. 2012;**3**(2):776-783

[84] Kulkarni SJ. Research on biocatalysts: A review. International Journal of Research. 2015;**2**(4):784-788

[85] Ramachandran V, Pujari N, Matey T, Kulkarni S. Enzymatic hydrolysis for glucose—A review. International Journal of Science, Engineering and Technology Research. 2013;**2**(10):1937-1942

[86] Fechter MH, Griengl H. Hydroxynitrile lyases: Biological sources and application as biocatalysts. Food Technology and Biotechnology. 2004;**42**(4):287-294

[87] Arumugam R, Manikandan M. Fermentation of pretreated hydrolyzates of banana and mango fruit wastes for ethanol production. Asian Journal of Experimental Biological Sciences. 2011;**2**(2):246-256

[88] Vilas MA. A critical overview of legal profile on solid waste management in India. International Journal of Research in Chemistry and Environment. 2015;**591**:1-16

[89] Nwachukwu NC, Orji FA, Ugbogu OC. Health care waste management-public health benefits, and the need for effective environmental regulatory surveillance in Federal Republic of Nigeria. In: Current Topics in Public Health. Rijeka: IntechOpen; 2013. pp. 149-180

[90] Amador AA. A hazardous waste management solution for Bogota. In: A Project Report Presented to the Faculty of the Department of Anthropology San José State University. 2010. pp. 1-264

[91] Kulkarni SJ. Review on solid waste management with emphasis on hazardous waste. International Journal of Research and Review. 2016;**3**(12):16-19

Chapter 7

An Empirical Study on Environmental Sustainability in Melaka City

Noor Mohammad

Abstract

Melaka is one of the most historic cities in Malaysia. It has been listed as a UNESCO Heritage Site since July 7, 2008. Once upon a time, it was also known as a trading center of Malaysia particularly in the Southeast Asian countries. But presently, her heritage has been facing numerous problems such as air pollution, water pollution, noise pollution, river pollution, unplanned urbanization, etc., based on several grounds including noncompliance with the existing sustainability laws, and therefore, some impacts such as ecological disruption, water-borne diseases, resource depletion, emission of greenhouse gases, etc. are observed in this city. This study, however, examines the environmental sustainability issues such as water pollution, climate change, food security, natural resource and heritage, biodiversity, etc. in Melaka City based on the primary and secondary sources consisting of 50 respondents in the different criteria such as lecturers, foreigners, workers, employees, common people, students, security personnel, etc. and finds that on an average the people in this city find around 60–70% sound environment and its sustainability prevailing in this city.

Keywords: environmental sustainability, Melaka City

1. Background

Melaka is one of the oldest states in Malaysia. The earliest written records of the country made reference to the Melaka Peninsula, since its founding, circa 1400, by a fleeing Sumatra Prince, Parameswara. The first of many foreign invasions of Melaka took place in 1511, when the Portuguese arrived.

The Portuguese were determined to control the East-West trade, so Melaka still retained its importance as a trade center until 1641 when the Portuguese surrendered Melaka to the Dutch. This was during the mid-1400s. The golden age of the Melaka Sultanate unfortunately lasted only for less than a century. Gradually, environmental problems have been occurring for a long time in the world. Melaka is not an exception to them due to severe negative impacts of human activities on this land [1] including flora and fauna [2]. Regarding water pollution, it is also acute in this city.

It is polluted in many ways that affects biodiversities on this land. Regarding noise pollution, it is also acute in many parts of the cities and towns in Malaysia and some effects and causes have also been identified. With regard to chemicals, it develops our agriculture but bears impacts on agriculture and facing numerous problems effects on the biodiversity [3]. The level of ground water is high, which creates environmental problems such as landslip, earthquake and deforestation. Filling of lakes, canals and wetlands has created environmental problems to the residential areas in this city.

It has become a problem and consequently, the fish biodiversities are missing in those areas. Wetlands in Malaysia have been facing large-scale destruction. A heavy deforestation is also identified with effects polyphones that have been used in the markets for shopping unprecedented which results in soil pollution.

Regarding land degradation, there are some factors such as unplanned irrigation systems, excessive use of chemical fertilizers, use of pesticides, earthquake, natural calamities, overpopulation, fragmentation of land, unhealthy drainage system, etc. that are held responsible for the environment.

Biodiversity degradation is also observed due to the use of biotechnology, genetically modified varieties, genetically engineered seeds, use of pesticides and chemical fertilizers and impacts of green house revolution, etc. With regard to bioprospecting, there is no specific legislation nationally but the State of Sarawak has made some initiatives in this regard. Inefficient solid waste management due to poor civic sense, inadequate facilities and inefficient management systems are also observed. Unplanned urbanization has been taking place in many cities in Malaysia due to lack of proper implementation of concerned rules and regulations and inadequate monitoring that bears tremendous stress on the physical environment of the city. Land has become inadequate for the urban people.

Regarding wastes, humans produce wastes that are hazardous and dangerous to both nature and human environment. No matter where it comes from, waste can be dangerous. One of the main causes of the abundance of hazardous waste is that people do not realize how large a problem it is [4].

Regarding different sector of environmental problems, it has been facing with numerous problems such as pollution, land degradation, deforestation, biodiversity degradation, depletion of environmental resources, wetland degradation, urban solid waste management, etc. In order to cope with these problems, the government has already passed some important laws and policies to protect the environment in Malaysia.

2. Literature review

There are some literatures on the different environmental sustainability in Melaka City that may be directly or indirectly relevant to this study. Some of the published literatures have also been discussed in order to identify the gaps of this study. According to the Singapore Journal [5], it discussed the marine pollution in the Straits of Malacca and Singapore. It also discusses the solutions to these problems.

Charles Sheppard and Jack Pearce Seas (2000) 'edited' at the Millennium: an Environmental Evaluation and has discussed on the Malacca Straits that have long been an important trade route linking in the Indian Ocean to the South China Sea and Pacific Ocean [6].

The author also discussed about the importance of the straits regarding renewable and non-renewable resources based on Malacca. Marine piracy and armed robbery against ships were also discussed in the Asia Information Sharing Center in Singapore focusing on a paper entitled Piracy and Armed Robbery in the Malacca Strait.

Some important websites such as www.Google search, Google Scholars, Emerald etc.; also discussed about the environmental pollution and sustainability issues in Melaka City.

The *UNDP-RIPP Natural Resource Management Country Studies Malaysian Report* prepared by Jannie Lasimbang has discussed the significance of the natural resource management and administration for protecting the environment [7].

The author finds that there are many environmental problems as stated earlier in this paper. We need to address these issues immediately as per the opinion of Chong stated in the paper titled [8].

The World Youth Foundation has discussed in an International Conference on the Environment and Disaster Management about the environmental protection and sustainable development in Malaysia dealing with common development, planning for environmental development, policy matters, institutional frameworks, ecology and equity along with the impacts of the international environmental treaties on the natural resource management and concerned development.

Azusa Ikeda has discussed about the natural ventilation for sustainability in a book titled "Introducing Natural Ventilation in Selected Malaysian Hotels for Environmental Sustainability" relating to the importance of Malay language [9].

Norfadhilah Mohd Ali discussed about the sustainability issues on the environmental conservation and development in "Sustainability of petroleum and environmental control in the Malaysian petroleum law deals with the existing Malaysian petroleum legislations and other relevant laws" on promoting sustainability of petroleum and environmental conservation [10].

The Malaysian Green Forum 2010 made a speech by Prime Minister, Dato; Sri Mohad Najib Bin Tun Haji Abdul Razak regarding the environmental issues in a holistic manner particularly, advancing for environmental and landscape issues in the country. He said that the biggest challenges that they are facing is the environmental awareness, renewable energy and cost-effective green technology.

Regarding existing environmental sustainability mechanisms, it is equally important at the national and international level in protecting the environment in Melaka city including Malaysia. As to effectiveness of laws, it is found that the laws are not so effective in their enforcement. The laws should be endowed with appropriate powers and responsibilities and should be acting as a form of international administrative agency.

This institution will play a fiduciary role in protecting the environment as supported by Alan E. Boyle, which is discussed in the saving the World [11]?

Regarding implementation and enforcement of international environmental law through international institutions, it is said that little attention is paid to the effectiveness of the new body of law.

Environmental laws are not self-executing and they cannot function in the absence of effective implementation. It is evident that the conservation laws are not carefully adapted to the distinctive political, social, economic, cultural and ecological conditions in each developing nation, which are likely to prove useless or worse.

Regarding inadequately designed legal mandates, it is also argued that most of the international environmental laws in developing states have been poorly conceived. They are overly general, deliberately ambiguous, often self-contradictory, excessively lenient and lacking in real teeth.

Moreover, inadequate political commitments and popular support are also observed in compliance with the laws and policies. Monitoring is also still lacking in this process. Unfortunately, environmental laws are only hortatory words unless they are implemented effectively, yet non-implementation, non-enforcement and non-compliance are so common that they must be viewed as the norm rather than exception in the great majority of nations.

3. Environmental sustainability

In order to explain the above topic, we need to explain the concept of environmental sustainability. It is based on around 76 variables. It includes the civil and political rights, legislations and policies, which are more likely to effectively address environmental challenges. It also includes the survey reports on environmental governance. The world environmental forum defines the environmental sustainability index as a derivative of five major components such as (i) current condition of the environmental system; (ii) pressure on the system; (iii) assessment of human vulnerability; (iv) social and institutional capacity; and (v) the level of participation in global environment stewardship.

Environmental sustainability is, in fact, closely related to the concept of democracy that is based on commonly accepted principles, such as freedom, equity, justice, transparency, accountability, good governance, rule of law, etc., to be ensured in all actions for achieving sustainable development. It is interlinked with the rights and duties of the flora and fauna that have to be ensured as well. It is a set of written and unwritten norms that is linked with the ecological balance in the governance of the institutions as well as the organizations around the globe to be ensured as well for all [12].

It is in fact intellectual governance of the environment for sustainable development. This index includes environmentally sound system that is reducing environmental stresses, reducing human vulnerability, social and institutional capacity and the global stewardship.

It includes several indicators of environmental sustainability that may be classified into several categories. Each indicator includes several variables. Sustainability encompasses nature, economy, society and well-being of individuals. It can be achieved through adopting some measures such as harmonization of standards, joint development of environmental management systems and collaborative capacity building projects.

It is in fact a tool for which environmental problems are solved in a scientific way by scientists in different fields of studies. It shows how environmental problems are identified and addressed also. It tries to ensure adequate environmental information, transparency and accountability, adequate capacity for credible enforcement and other policies that may promote better environmental performance of the activities done by the concerned institutions at home and abroad [13].

The environmental governance structures in Asia and the South Asian countries are frequently being changed. It involves three distinctive levels where the operational entities are primarily international governing bodies, donor agencies, international NGOs and government.

At the national level, many new environmental laws, policies, programs and institutional changes are being made.

At the regional and international levels, a significant number of the environmental initiatives are undertaken by the international intergovernmental bodies, international nongovernmental organizations and also many other environmental organizations including the international environmental laws and institutions to develop and conserve the environment at different levels in the globe.

But it faces incoherence, lack of co-operation and coordination, inefficiency and lack of implementation for ensuring environmental governance. It needs the coordination and collaboration in between the levels of operations. Some environmental organizations including the European Union, the IUCN, PADELIA, WWF, UNITAR, UNEP, etc. have been playing a significant role in this regard. However, the European Union wants to encourage the civil society, bottom-down method and the principles of good governance for assessing environmental governance. In the

ASEAN countries, it is found that the nongovernmental organizations and the civil society organizations are rendering the services in the area of environmental monitoring, management, poverty alleviation, greening programs, environmental education, etc. In the South Asian and South East ASEANS countries, it is found in the same kind. Particularly, the charters of the different organizations including the UNO and the international environmental laws have been playing a significant role in the protection and conservation of the environment in these regions.

4. The role of environmental sustainability mechanisms

Let us discuss about the role of the existing environmental sustainability mechanisms passed by the government of Malaysia relating to the protection of the environment in Melaka City of Malaysia.

4.1 The role of environmental law and policy

The Environmental law and policy of Malaysia bears a significant role in protecting the environment of this city. At present, environmental problems are largely found in this country including Melaka City supported by Suzanna Mohamed Isa, such as air pollution, water pollution, exploitation of natural resources, etc. [14]. In order to sustain the quality environment and coping with the environmental problems, the Government of Malaysia has passed some important environmental laws and policies such as the Environment Quality Regulations 1989, the Environmental Quality Order 1989, the Protection of Wildlife Act, the National Forestry Act 1984, the Fisheries Act 1985, the National Parks Act 1980, some common laws and principles along with international environmental obligations, etc. [15].

4.2 The role of constitutional guidelines

Regarding the role of the constitution of Malaysia in protecting the environment, there is no direct constitutional provision on the environmental issues in Malaysia [16]. The Malaysian Constitution discussed very precisely the powers and functions of the Federal Government as well as the State Government as per the provisions of Part VI of the Constitutions. Moreover, there are three legislative lists in the constitution that are given to the Federal and State Governments for making their legislations and Ninth Schedule and a concurrent list where either the Federal or the State Government can make laws. In the meantime, some states including Melaka passed some laws relating to the protection and conservation of the environment as per the guidelines of the constitution. It is mentioned here that these lists bear effects indirectly on the environment.

4.3 The role of government

The government has been playing significantly their role as per the guidelines of the constitution. The government may carry out their duties in many ways for the Federal and State Government with regard to making their legislations the State Role have been implementing many issues related to the environmental development. The Malaysian Government has been encouraging environmental nongovernmental organizations throughout the country to make the country green for attaining environmental sustainability in the country.

4.4 The role of judiciary

It is stated that there is no specific and direct environmental court in Malaysia to protect the environment. But the general court is quite active dealing with the environmental issues based on the constitutional obligations and interpretation along with the English Common Law Principles under the judiciary of Malaysia covering Melaka City. The High Court and the Supreme Court of Malaysia may deal with these issues. Some judicial decisions were found between 1992 and 2002 dealing with the environmental issues in Malaysia. In the constitution, there is no specific article dealing with the clean environment. It is not defined in the constitution. The Indian Constitution clearly mentioned about the right to clean environment, which we may include in our constitution. A decision in Malaysian Court may be pointed out here regarding the environment as:

> *"...The expression 'life' appearing in the Article 5(1) of the constitution of Malaysia does not refer to mere existence. It incorporates all those facets that are an integral part of life itself and those matters which go to form the quality of life. Of these are the rights to seek and be engaged in lawful and gainful employment and to receive those benefits that our society has to offer its members. It includes the right to live in a reasonably healthy and pollution free environment."*

In this regard, the Bakun Dam case may also be added here as follows:

> *"...They will suffer deprivation of their livelihood and cultural heritage by reason of the Project... This complaint certainly comes within the scope of the expression 'life' in Article 5(1) of the federal Constitution. For where there is deprivation of livelihood or one's way of life, that is to say, one's culture, there is deprivation of life itself... However, in the present case, as earlier observed, the State of Sarawak will extinguish the respondent's rights in accordance with the provisions of existing written law obtaining in the State... Since, in this instance, life is being deprived in accordance with an existing and valid law, the requirements of Article 5(1) are met. It may be certainly said that the following case laws bear importance directly or indirectly on the environment."*

4.5 Some case laws

Some judicial decisions have also been made directly or indirectly on the environmental issues in Malaysia. Some of the cases are given here to understand their role on the environmental issues such as the Rural Legislation and Entitlement Kendra Dehradun and others Vs State of U.P. and Others (1985) 2 SCC 431, Devaki Nandan Pandey V. Union of India and Others (1985) 3 SCC 614, Tan Tek Seng V. Suruhanjaya Perkhidmatan Pendidikan (1996)1 MLJ 288, Kettua Pengarah Jabatan Alam Sekitar & Anor vs. Kajing Tubek & Ors (1997) 3 MLJ 23, Government of Malaysia vs. Lim kit Siang, United Engineers (M) Berhad vs. Lim Kit Siang (1988) 2 MLJ 12, The Malaysian Vermicelli Manufacturers (Melaka), Sdn Bhd vs. PP (2001) 7 CLJ, etc.

5. Empirical results and discussion

The discussion and results of the study are based on the above methodology and are presented below.

Environmental issues	Minimum	Maximum	Average (%)	Std. deviation	Median
Access to clean drinking water	50.00	100.00	80.10	10.41	80.00
Access to sanitation/clean environment	30.00	100.00	70.96	10.45	80.00
Forest areas for good environment	40.00	100.00	70.62	10.33	70.00
Wetland/ponds/haors/beels for fisheries	30.00	100.00	60.88	10.25	70.00
Amusement/park/gardening for recreation	40.00	100.00	70.26	10.36	70.00
Car parking facilities	20.00	100.00	60.96	10.51	70.00
Motor vehicles for pollution	50.00	100.00	70.32	10.20	70.00
Population in Melaka good for environment	30.00	100.00	70.58	20.11	80.00
Urban infrastructure facilities	40.00	100.00	70.86	10.24	80.00
Access to gas for cooking	60.00	100.00	80.88	10.25	90.00
Quality medical services	50.00	100.00	80.06	10.03	80.00
Fresh food in Melaka	40.00	100.00	80.34	10.18	80.50
Electricity	40.00	100.00	90.26	10.30	100.00
The price of daily commodities friendly with the people	30.00	100.00	70.38	10.56	80.00
Poverty range friendly to Melaka (the poor/the rich)	30.00	100.00	40.90	10.77	40.00
Waste dumping system	30.00	100.00	60.90	10.46	70.00
Diversified culture	50.00	100.00	70.76	10.46	80.00
Law & Order situation in Melaka	20.00	100.00	70.04	10.48	70.00
Local administration in Melaka	40.00	100.00	60.98	10.43	70.00
Availability of daily commodities for shopping	50.00	100.00	70.46	10.28	70.00
Income & expenses friendly with the people	50.00	100.00	60.84	10.20	70.00
Relationship between foreigners & local people	30.00	100.00	60.92	10.75	70.00
Misdeeds (robbery, dacoits/theft), etc.	20.00	100.00	50.02	20.25	40.50
Security to the residential areas	30.00	100.00	70.46	10.50	70.50
Accountability in administration	50.00	100.00	70.70	10.14	80.00
Transportation facilities	30.00	100.00	70.50	10.61	70.00
Quality education in Melaka	30.00	100.00	70.16	10.78	70.00
Corruption in Melaka	20.00	100.00	50.48	20.51	40.50
Natural environment	40.00	100.00	70.98	10.31	80.00
Access to justice	50.00	100.00	70.48	10.11	70.00
Using of polythene (harmful for environment)	40.00	100.00	70.68	10.39	80.00

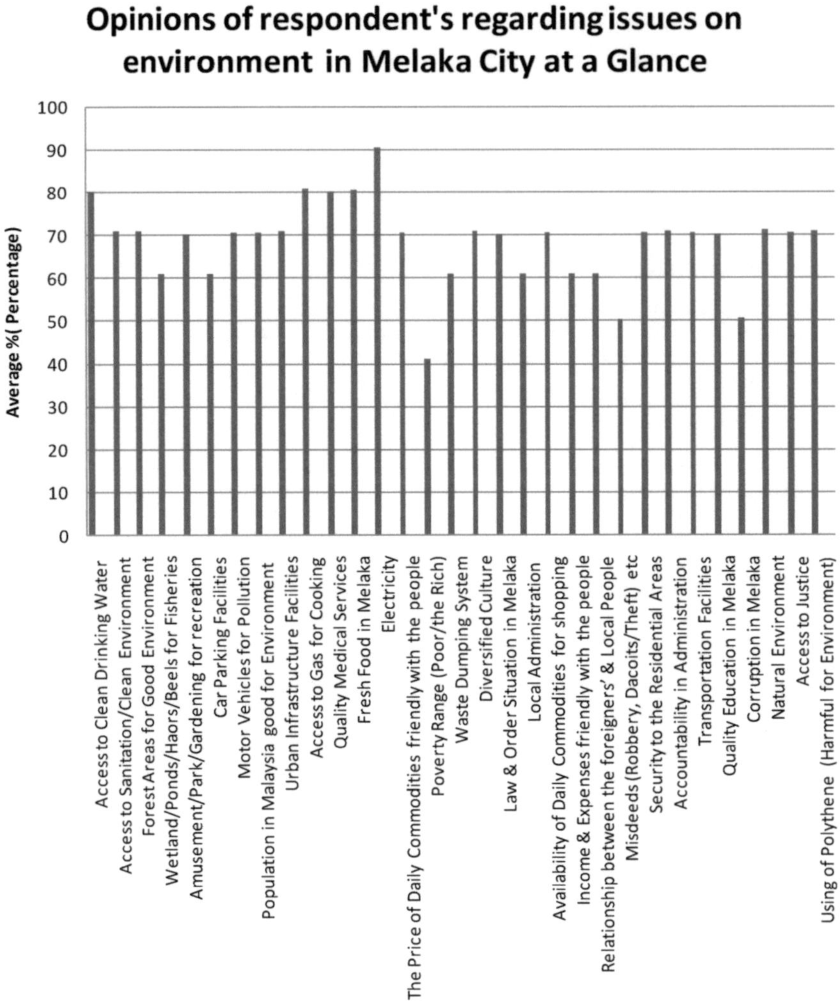

From the above chart, the study finds that the above services as identified in Melaka City are very friendly to the environment in this city. A discussion on the empirical results has been discussed as follows:

1. Access to clean drinking water: About 80% of the people are satisfied with pure drinking water in Melaka City.

2. Access to clean environment: In Melaka City, 71% of respondents think that they are living and enjoying clean environment.

3. Forest areas for good environment: About 71% of the people think that they have forest areas for maintaining good environment.

4. Wetland/ponds/haors/beels for fisheries: Among all respondents, around 61% think that the wetlands produce good environment.

5. Amusement/park/gardening for recreation: In the survey, 70.26% of the respondents think that they have amusement facilities, like parks, in the Melaka area.

6. Car parking facilities: In Malaysia, particularly in Melaka City, 61% of the people think that they have car parking facilities.

7. Parking facilities: About 61% of the people responded that parking facilities in Malacca are quite limited, especially during the weekend, when there are many tourists in Malacca.

8. Motor vehicles for pollution: In the survey, 70.32% of people felt that in Malacca there is environmental pollution.

9. Population in Melaka good for environment: About 71% of people think that they are healthy due to the nature of the environment in Melaka City.

10. Urban infrastructure facilities: Good urban infrastructure in Melaka City was supported by 71% of all respondents.

11. Access to gas for cooking: 81% of the total respondents felt there is adequate access to gas for cooking for their daily life.

12. Quality medical services: About 86% of Melaka City residents reported quality medical services.

13. Fresh food in Melaka: In Melaka City, 80% of respondents reported having fresh food.

14. Electricity: The availability of electricity in Melaka City is 90%.

15. The price of daily commodities friendly with the people: Some 70% of people in Melaka City think that the price of daily commodities is friendly.

16. Poverty range friendly to Melaka (the poor/the rich): Only 41% of the people surveyed thought that the poverty range (the poor/the rich) is friendly.

17. Waste dumping system: In the survey, 61% people reported having waste dumping system in Melaka City.

18. Diversified culture: In Melaka City, around 71% of respondents indicated that they have a diversified culture.

19. Law and order situation in Melaka: About 70% of people in Melaka City think that they feel better regarding the law and order situation in this city.

20. Local administration in Melaka: Some 61% of people in the sample respondents are satisfied with the local administration.

21. Availability of daily commodities for shopping: Around 71% of people reported that they have daily need commodities available for shopping in this city.

22. Income and expenses friendly with the people: The income and expenses are friendly in the city as reported by 61% of the survey respondents in Melaka City.

23. Relationship between foreigners and local people: A majority of people (61% of total) in Melaka City find the existence of good relationship between foreigners and local people.

25. Misdeeds (robbery, dacoits/theft), etc.: About half the respondents acknowledged some misdeeds.

26. Security to the residential areas: About 71% of the people in this area think that they are secure in the residential areas.

27. Accountability in administration: Majority (71%) of people responded that the administration maintains accountability in their actions.

28. Transportation facilities: Satisfaction with transportation facilities by people in the Melaka City was reported by 70.5% of the total.

29. Quality education in Melaka: People in this area think that they have 70% quality education.

30. Corruption in Melaka: About half the respondent of the survey felt that there are corrupt activities in this area.

31. Natural environment: Natural environments were appreciated by 71% of respondents in Melaka City.

32. Access to justice: About 70% of the people in the sample think that they have access to justice.

33. Using of polythene (harmful for environment): A majority of people in Melaka City (71% of total) think that using of polythene is harmful to their environment.

6. Recommendations and conclusion

Environmental sustainability is one of the burning issues in Melaka City. In order to sustain the environment of Melaka City, this study finds that there are some important tools such as strict application of the rule of law, improvement of the respective institutional capacity, maintaining coordination with the respective departments, and enforcement of the existing sustainability laws and policies, focusing on the implementation of the findings of the existing research including this work.

Acknowledgements

We would also like to express our sincere gratitude to all concerned authors and authorities at home and abroad.